Early Muir Invention —
Measured Atmospheric Conditions

Hickory Hill Farm, Wisconsin

Athens, Georgia

Bonaventure Cemetery,
Savannah, Georgia

JOHN MUIR'S WILD AMERICA

By Tom Melham
Photographed by Farrell Grehan

Prepared by the Special Publications Division
National Geographic Society, Washington, D. C.

JOHN MUIR'S WILD AMERICA

By Tom Melham
National Geographic Staff
Photographed by Farrell Grehan
Paintings by H. Tom Hall

Published by
The National Geographic Society
Melvin M. Payne, *President*
Melville Bell Grosvenor, *Editor-in-Chief*
Gilbert M. Grosvenor, *Editor*

Prepared by
The Special Publications Division
Robert L. Breeden, *Editor*
Donald J. Crump, *Associate Editor*
Philip B. Silcott, *Senior Editor*
William R. Gray, *Managing Editor*
Louisa Magzanian, Wendy W. Cortesi, *Research*

Illustrations and Design
Steve Raymer, *Picture Editor*
Ursula Perrin Vosseler, *Art Director*
Marie A. Bradby, Linda McCarter Bridge,
   Wendy W. Cortesi, Jacqueline Geschickter,
   P. Tyrus Harrington, Margaret McKelway
   Johnson, Tom Melham, Judith E. Rinard,
   Picture Legends
Tibor Toth, *Calligraphy*
John D. Garst, Jr., Margaret A. Deane, Victor
   J. Kelley, Nancy Schweickart, Milda R.
   Stone, *Map Research, Design, and Production*

Production and Printing
Robert W. Messer, *Production Manager*
George V. White, *Assistant Production Manager*
Raja D. Murshed, June L. Graham, *Production
   Assistants*
John R. Metcalfe, *Engraving and Printing*
Jane H. Buxton, Stephanie S. Cooke, Mary C.
   Humphreys, Suzanne J. Jacobson, Sandra Lee
   Matthews, Virginia A. McCoy, Selina R. M.
   Patton, Christine A. Roberts, Marilyn L.
   Wilbur, *Staff Assistants*
Virginia S. Thompson, *Index*

Library of Congress CIP Data: page 199

**Its wings as radiant as stained glass, a monarch
butterfly climbs a blue curls plant in Florida.
All of nature captivated John Muir: "The universe would be incomplete ... without the
smallest transmicroscopic creature...."**

**Overleaf: Solitary Jeffrey pine juts above the
summit of Sentinel Dome in Yosemite National
Park, California—a wilderness that John Muir
helped preserve. Page 1: White hair and beard
frame the face of Muir, America's wilderness
sage. Bookbinding: Muir in a reflective mood.**

OVERLEAF: NATIONAL GEOGRAPHIC PHOTOGRAPHER STEVE RAYMER; PAGE 1:
PAINTING BY HERBERT A. COLLINS, SR., NPS, MUIR WOODS; ENDPAPERS: LISA
BIGANZOLI; BOOKBINDING: PAINTING BY SAM WILSON, FLYING SPUR PRESS COLLECTION

CONTENTS

Prologue

JOHN MUIR: NATURE'S VISIONARY

"The more savage and chilly and storm-chafed the mountains, the finer the glow on their faces," wrote John Muir of such rugged landscapes as Admiralty Island in Alaska. Muir, who portrayed himself (above) as a wild mountain man with piercing eyes, became one of America's most thoughtful, eloquent, and wide-ranging naturalists.

THE LEAN, BEARDED MOUNTAINEER woke early. Alone in the white silence of a new-fallen snow, he set out for a distant ridge towering above California's Yosemite Valley. Waist-deep drifts robed the countryside, imprisoning his legs. At times he sank almost out of sight. Yet onward he climbed, hour after hour, tirelessly as a mountain goat.

A desire to stand on the summit and rejoice in nature's magnificence fired his uphill struggle. Less than an hour before sundown, his goal lay just a few hundred feet above him. But suddenly, he heard a rumble. He looked up and watched as the snow above him crumbled and slipped downward, shattering the silence with that dull, terrifying roar most dreaded by mountain men. Avalanche!

Instantly, the climber was hurtling toward the valley on a crashing torrent of white, tossed about like a leaf in a gale. Amazingly, he was not buried alive. A last-second impulse to spread-eagle himself enabled him to ride atop the snow. When the avalanche smashed into the valley floor about a minute later, he emerged, miraculously, "on top of the crumpled pile without a bruise or scar."

One such hair-raising brush with death can leave a person in shock—or at least convinced he should avoid mountain climbing. But this stalwart mountaineer could scarcely contain his ecstasy: "Elijah's flight in a chariot of fire could hardly have been more gloriously exciting," he exulted. Here was a man who loved nature! His astonishing ride on what he called "a milky way of snow-stars" was no ordinary adventure. Nor was he an ordinary man. He was, of course, John Muir.

Father of Yosemite, savior of the sequoias, tireless priest at nature's shrine—John Muir made the American wilderness his lifework. More than any other man, this eloquent naturalist, writer, explorer, and pioneer ecologist popularized the cause of conservation—at a time when national resources seemed inexhaustible, and the wilderness was being exploited. He helped found the Sierra Club, Western spearhead of the conservation movement, and served as its first president. He explored and glowingly described Alaska's Glacier Bay. He discovered new plants and insects, some of which now bear his name, as do many schools, lakes, mountains, trails, and national preserves throughout the country. Today, more place-names in California honor Muir than anyone else.

In his own lifetime—he died in 1914 at age 76—Muir drew recognition for his wilderness expertise from presidents and poets alike. Ralph Waldo Emerson considered him one of the greatest men he had ever met.

Yet John Muir always retained a rustic modesty and humor. A newspaper reporter once asked the sage of wilderness to define his occupation. "Tramp," Muir replied. "I'm seventy-four, and still good at it."

Indeed he was. To the end, Muir remained a champion walker. Usually alone, he rambled thousands of miles across America's most challenging terrain, from swamplands of coastal Florida to his beloved mountains, the Sierra Nevada of California. He knew the gentle beauty of Washington's Olympic Peninsula, the colors of Arizona's Grand Canyon, the barren rock and ice of Alaska's fiords. In many ways, Muir was as rugged as the lands he tramped. Preparing for a trip usually meant only that he would "throw some tea and bread in an old sack and jump over the back fence."

A distinctive individualist, he opposed war — even during the Civil War, when most of his contemporaries enlisted. He also shunned money, though he saved many thousands of dollars during a decade as a California fruit grower. His most treasured commodity was *time* — time to pore over a leaf or trace a glacier's trail, time to ramble, time to write and sketch and study, time to learn nature's varied wilderness lessons.

"I have not yet in all my wanderings found a single person so free as myself," he confided to a friend. Of all American naturalists, Muir was the wildest; he was also the most active, the most self-reliant, and the most persuasive, probably because his knowledge came from nature, not simply from books.

In endless pursuit of that wisdom, John Muir disdained creature comforts, preferring instead to live on "essences and crumbs." His beard and hair grew shaggy; his clothes became equally unkempt. But Muir's roughhewn exterior and free-form life-style never deterred him from success. He achieved what many aspire to but so few attain: He lived his own life, following the dictates of his heart for good or ill — and yet he still wrought lasting changes in the world.

Whether camping among the sequoias or scaling an unclimbed peak, Muir hewed to a diet of solo trips, continually exposing himself to what others might consider unthinkable dangers: avalanches, bears, frostbite, isolation, fierce storms. But to Muir, such dangers were merely grand opportunities to explore the mysterious natural world that served him as both laboratory and temple. When a winter gale descended on the Yuba River valley of northern California, he "lost no time in pushing out into the woods to enjoy it." Nature's raw power entranced him with scenes of "pines six feet in diameter bending like grasses." Falling trees crashed about him. "The air was mottled with pine-tassels and bright green plumes, that went flashing past in the sunlight like birds pursued." But that was not enough; the wild-spirited Muir needed to immerse himself in the storm's very heart "and get my ear close to the Æolian music" — and so he climbed a hundred-foot Douglas fir, its wind-bullied top "rocking and swirling in wild ecstasy."

Here he spent much of the afternoon, captivated by "so noble an exhilaration of motion." Yet Muir's senses tuned in to

the sublime as well as to the terrifying. From his lofty perch he sorted out faint fragrances borne on the raging gusts. "Winds are advertisements of all they touch," he noted, his nose telling him that "this wind came first from the sea, rubbing against its fresh, briny waves, then distilled through the redwoods, threading rich ferny gulches, and spreading itself in broad undulating currents over many a flower-enameled ridge of the coast mountains, then . . . into these piny woods with the varied incense gathered by the way." Such sensitivity of feeling and thought deepened throughout Muir's life, reflecting a delightfully child-like wonderment, not only in storms but in anything wild. A single flower, a bumblebee, a frothy waterfall all were to him great marvels, each a tiny but indispensable part of nature's grand harmony.

And so he never tired of climbing the next ridge—or of crusading for its preservation. In his day, many people considered the wilds valuable only for their economic rewards. John Muir began to open their eyes.

"The clearest way into the Universe is through a forest wilderness," he would preach. "Climb the mountains and get their good tidings. Nature's peace will flow into you as sunshine flows into trees. The winds will blow their own freshness into you, and the storms their energy, while cares will drop off like autumn leaves."

Such words hold special relevance in today's increasingly crowded and urbanized world, where civilization steadily encroaches upon wilderness. But the number of Muir enthusiasts is on the rise, and they are rediscovering his pioneering insights into untamed nature.

Though change has overtaken the land he knew, much of Muir's America exists, free and wild, even today. It is this America that he championed, this America that inspired his richest writings and most important achievements. By focusing both on nature's awful grandeur and its gentle magic, he realized that the earth is even now in the process of creation, with every atom of the cosmos bonded to the next. "Everything is so inseparably united," he wrote.

Unlike many naturalists who praised only certain geographic areas, Muir lauded the universe. His dynamic interest in all things, large and small, adds vitality to his writings. It also links him solidly to the science of togetherness—ecology—a term coined in Muir's lifetime but only recently brought into the layman's lexicon by a mushrooming awareness of earth's fragility. Even today, John Muir is far from outdated. His philosophy of permitting the wilderness to remain wild seems more timely now than when first proposed. One need only enter a virgin forest and feel nature's peace "flow into you as sunshine flows into trees" to know that the shaggy, baggy-trousered "tramp" was right.

"There is nothing like a storm," bellows John Muir, after scaling a Douglas fir during a gale in northern California. Clinging "with muscles firm braced, like a bobolink on a reed," he drank in the "wild exuberance of light and motion" for hours, certain that "on such occasions, Nature has always something rare to show us." Throughout his life, Muir sought to experience all facets of nature, from the violent to the sublime.

"I... am always glad to touch the living rock again and dip my head in high mountain sky."

Morning sun bursts behind an exultant rock climber atop a pinnacle in California's Sierra Nevada. Thousands of hikers and climbers penetrate the lofty peaks of the Sierra each year to regain, like Muir, their "wilderness health." Muir's ceaseless love of high country fired a determination to scale as many peaks as he could—the Cascade and Coast Ranges, the Olympic Mountains, and the glaciered crags of southeastern Alaska. But more than any other range, Muir loved the granite-bound Sierra.

GALEN ROWELL

"The clearest way into the Universe

Spires of a serene woodland cathedral, giant sequoias in Sequoia National Park, California, reac

is through a forest wilderness."

heavenward. Muir felt at peace in such enclaves, and he worked to preserve them for others.

"...if a war of races should occur between the wild beasts and Lord Man, I would be tempted to sympathize with the bears."

Chest-deep in an icy Alaskan stream, a brown bear devours a humpback salmon. Muir loved all wilderness creatures for their freedom and closeness to nature's heart. The grasshopper—"the mountain's merriest child"—ranked among his favorites. He laced the margins of a letter (opposite) with sketches of its tracks.

(Consider the grasshoppers how they grow & go)

Yosemite Valley
Sunday Sep 27th 1874

Dear Mrs Carr.

I have been dawn bathing in the Ganges. I wonder if I will ever know another river like this. After splashing & laving in the spangling crystal I swam across to examine a section of the bank & found charred bark ten feet below lake & flood deposits. In a vertical portion of the bank I discovered two small frogs of a new species each snugly nestled in a dainty nitch from whence they could look out over the water. They are not water frogs however. I swam over with them in my hand holding them aloft & when I ducked them they made a great nervous ado. I have them in my room hoping they may sing like crickets or tree frogs for me in the night.

In walking over the pebbles I received some tingling lessons meant drift formations upon the soles of my feet. The wind sifted deliciously through my raising flesh & thrilled every fiber. The afternoon sun shimmered upon the glossy poplars bright as upon the rippled currents of the river. A thicket of tall waving golden rods warms the south bank & the whole valley is full of light like a lake in wh one instinctively laves & winnows as if it were water.

I chased a grasshopper & finally wearied the lusty fellow & made him attempt to fly over the river into wh he fell & I ran out & captured him before any of the trouts. Another larger one flew up wh I also succeeded in driving into the river but just as I got within arms length a trout caught him by the legs & drew him down. I clipt the wings of the first & carried him to my room to experiment upon his habits & movements. Here is an exact copy of his walking embroidered track wh I got by compelling him to walk across a plateful of fine sand in my room. I showed the original track to an Indian but he only grinned & didnt sake. Blacks chinaman was also puzzled, & thought it might be writing. Billy Simms happened along & inquired for Kellogg & Keith. I showed him the track & he guessed it might be that of a tarantula or centipede. No 1 in the fig is made by the middle feet No 2 by the front feet & No 3 by the feet of the big jumping pair. Fig 4 is made by his body & is more or less continuous according to his weariness or the depth his feet sink in the sand. The three figures at the head are copies of the tracks he makes in jumping. First are made by the front pair, 2 the second & the third & 4 by the body in crouching.

It is beautiful is it not & the track embroidery of the gray lizards is still more beautiful.

"...glaciers...are only streams of closely compacted snow-crystals."

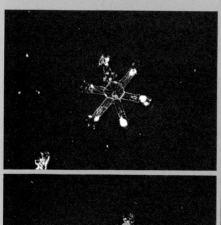

Contorted by melting, icebergs spawned by glaciers float in Alaska's Tracy Arm—a fiordlike inlet of the sea. In 1880, Muir canoed among such ice floes while exploring the glaciers of Alaska. Glaciologist as well as mountaineer, he early recognized the geologic force of ice in shaping the peaks and canyons of both Alaska and the West: "...Nature chose for a tool not

the earthquake or lightning . . . but the tender snow-flowers noiselessly
falling through unnumbered centuries. . . . Strong only by force of numbers,
they carried away entire mountains, particle by particle, block by block,
and cast them into the sea. . . ." Magnification reveals the fragile beauty of
snowflakes (opposite) — a contrast to the rumbling power of glaciers.

"*How deeply with beauty is beauty overlaid!*"

"There is not a fragment in all nature," Muir believed, "for every relative fragment of one thing is a full harmonious unit in itself." Details of nature (clockwise, from above) reflect his words: the ice-dappled bank of a quiet river; the outspread segments of a palm leaf; the graceful plumage on the wing of a ruffed grouse; and the convoluted designs on a glaciated rock.

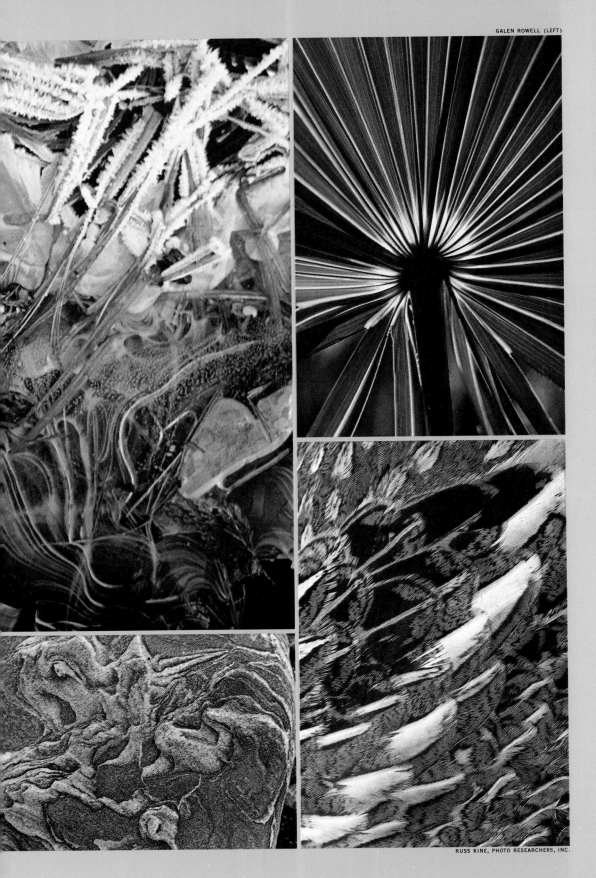

21

"Light. I know not a single word fine enough for Light... holy, beamless, bodiless, inaudible floods of Light."

Shafts of dawning sunlight pierce a thick blanket of fog enveloping trees along the coast of the Pacific Ocean in Washington. Throughout his 76 years, Muir maintained a youthful enthusiasm for the simple majesties of the wilderness—the trees, the rocks, the plants, the animals. "Go to Nature's school—the one true University," he advised.

1

EARLY
PATHS
TO
WILDERNESS

Crumbled ruins of Dunbar Castle, play-ground for young John Muir, command grassy cliffs near Dunbar, Scotland— Muir's birthplace. Living there for his first 11 years, Muir discovered a "natural inherited wildness" in his blood. After moving to America, he found he had a genius for inventing, which resulted in such designs as the hickory clock (above), shaped like the scythe of Father Time.

AMERICA'S APOSTLE OF WILDERNESS blazed his first trails in Scotland, not the United States; and instead of mountain wilds, he tramped the cobbled streets of Dunbar, a coastal town east of Edinburgh. Here, the hardy, scrappy, eldest son of grain merchant Daniel Muir spent his first 11 years, eating green apples and squeezing through neighbors' hedges.

Even in Dunbar, John Muir found "no lack of wildness." A sprouting seed, a robin's nest, the simplest touch of nature fascinated him. So did the surrounding countryside: "With red-blooded playmates, wild as myself, I loved to wander in the fields to hear the birds sing, and along the seashore to gaze and wonder at the shells and seaweeds, eels and crabs. . . ."

Today, fields golden with ripening barley and wheat still surround the town. Gulls ride the winds on motionless wings, and bumblebees drone from blossom to blossom, their hind legs clumped with yellow pollen balls. The North Sea's rocky shoreline still beckons Dunbar's youngsters, as it did John Muir nearly a century and a half ago. They sail toy boats and poke about tidal pools for "grannies"—sea urchins. And only two blocks from the surf stands a square, clay-tiled house at 128 High Street, where Muir was born.

A dry cleaner's establishment has displaced Daniel Muir's shop on the ground floor. But the third and topmost story, where his family lived, shows few changes today. Aged floorboards of random widths run between thick plastered walls. The original entrance—on a narrow passageway off High Street —still serves the present tenant, who climbs gray sandstone steps so worn they seem to sag under their own weight. Even spots repaired by stone patches bear the mark of countless feet padding "up and doon."

Soon after John's birth, the family moved to a larger house next door—the scene of many childhood pranks that busied Muir in his early years. One blustery night, he ventured outside his dormer window to hang from its sill by a single finger, a feat immediately imitated by younger brother David. Then John, his nightgown ballooning in the wind, scrambled spiderlike up the steep incline to the peak of the roof. After his dangerous return, Davie made the same ascent—only to find he could not get down. John then stood on the sill, one hand clinging to the window, the other directing his brother. When Davie's unsure feet came within reach, John grabbed them and hauled him to safety—quite an exploit for a lad not even in his teens!

Returning to Dunbar some 50 years later, Muir visited his former home and concluded that, despite all his mountaineering in the intervening years, "what I had done in daring boyhood was now beyond my skill."

I have seen the Muir house and looked at its roof and cannot understand how Muir scaled it at any age. But climbing was always one of his favorite pastimes; feet that later tramped the wild American West earned their first blisters here, and on the red sandstone ruins of Dunbar Castle, which still dominates the harbor. This strategic fortress once protected Mary Queen of Scots and, earlier, the romantic "Black Agnes"—a swarthy countess still remembered in local schools for rallying the defenders during an English siege in 1338. Two centuries later, the castle's battlements were breached—not by war but by Parliamentary edict. The castle became a children's playground. As Muir recalled, "We tried to see who could climb highest on the crumbling peaks and crags, and took chances that no cautious mountaineer would try."

Today, storms from the North Sea batter the castle's ghostly foundations, and weeds steadily encroach upon shattered walls. "No Trespassing" signs warn climbers away, but still some daredevil youths scramble up the stones, which crumble like stale cake. "It's good fun, that," one lad commented as he started up a magnificently derelict wall. Sixty seconds later, he stood victoriously at the top.

"Can ye come up? Aye, let's see how good ye are," he challenged me with purebred Scots daring. That dare—and a desire to follow Muir's every footstep—doomed my better judgment, and I soon found myself laboring up the ancient stones. Studying each for strength as well as handholds, I eased into a steady cycle of gripping, stepping, and lifting myself to ever-higher niches. I soon made the top—about as surprised as my comrade.

"Ye're a real danger-man," he applauded. I savored the triumph. No wonder Muir loved to climb!

Even as a lad, Muir grew so confident of his climbing skills that "when I first heard of hell from a servant girl . . . I always insisted that I could climb out of it. I imagined it was only a sooty pit with stone walls like those of the castle. . . ."

Climbs and other feats of daring were called "scootchers" by Muir, who pulled enough of them to win repeated lashings and stern pronouncements from his Bible-preaching father: "The very deevil's in that boy!" Muir's mother, Ann, however, remained calm. Her quiet humor, her yen for drawing, poetry, and nature would later blossom in her eldest son. But early on, the "deevil" ruled John—and other young Scots.

"After attaining the manly, belligerent age of five or six years," he admits, "very few of my schooldays passed without a fist fight. . . . To be a 'gude fechter' was our highest ambition. . . . The moment our master disappeared . . . every scholar left his seat and his lessons, jumped on top of the benches and desks or crawled beneath them, tugging, rolling, wrestling, accomplishing in a minute a depth of disorder and din unbelievable save by a Scottish scholar."

Within an hour of my arrival in Dunbar, I witnessed the first of several schoolboy fights, all near Muir's favorite battleground—Davel Brae, a hill between the harbor and the school.

The quarrel began as a rather formalized shoving contest. Then one boy smacked his opponent with a dead herring left from the morning catch. The other, his curly hair now sequined with fish scales, did the same. Tempers glowed as comrades egged on the pair. Finally, eyes afire, the rivals squared off, one swinging his fists like a windmill while the other jabbed—but they stood, almost comically, too far apart to make contact. Fists furiously lashed empty air. Then the Windmill stepped forward, his arms churning blindly, until one punch plowed into the Jabber's eye. Pain overswelled pride; anguished tears soon ended the fight.

The fierceness of this brief bout made me wonder out loud if the two were sworn enemies. *"Them?"* asked a bystander. "Na, na. They're just brithers."

A few minutes later, the Jabber was all smiles and laughs, kidded out of his defeat by friends. And only a few minutes after that, two other combatants were scrapping.

During this second battle, a 7-year-old, drawn by my interest in the fights, proudly strolled over to show me his scarred and lumpy head, splotched with bald spots where new skin had failed to sprout hair. "What happened to you?" I asked.

"Fell off the roof," came his offhand reply, full of pride at the attention his injury commanded. "I was up there playin' and me friends pushed me doon." His voice bore no twinge of bitterness. Like Muir, this 20th-century "fechter" scorned such traits as weakness.

In Muir's day, parental whippings often rewarded fighters whether they won or lost. But whippings were often "without avail; fighting went on without the slightest abatement, like natural storms; for no punishment less than death could quench the ancient inherited belligerence burning in our pagan blood." Even when they weren't battling each other, they often got beatings. Scotland's "whole educational system was founded on leather," Muir complained. So was home life. By the age of 11, he had learned almost the entire Bible "by heart and sore flesh." This was to please his devout and strict father, who also kept meals light because he felt that a spartan diet nurtured the soul.

Still, the indomitable Johnnie Muir "grew up savagely strong," acquiring an endurance that would see him through a lifetime of mountain storms and glacial rambles. As if his regular punishments were not enough to bear, he indulged in stoic games of "shin-battering shinny," in which schoolboys thrashed each other's legs until one gave up in pain. They considered the ignominy of defeat worse than any physical discomfort.

And yet nature, not competition, remained Muir's prime love, and Davie's as well. John recalled of his youth, "... like devout martyrs of wildness, we stole away to the seashore or the green, sunny fields with almost religious regularity.... Wildness was ever sounding in our ears...."

In school, John began learning about natural history; he was excited by John James Audubon's tales of American wildlife. And then one night Daniel Muir came home with a stunning message for his children: "Bairns, you needna learn your lessons the nicht, for we're gan to America the morn!"

Davie and John erupted with glee, their soaring imaginations envisioning America's "boundless woods full of mysterious good things; trees full of sugar, growing in ground full of gold; hawks, eagles, pigeons, filling the sky; millions of birds' nests, and no gamekeepers to stop us in all the wild, happy land." They left Scotland as "care-free as thistle seeds."

The Muirs emigrated in 1849 — the year of the California gold rush — but in search of land, not gold. Daniel sold his grain shop and vacated his seat on Dunbar's town council solely for the opportunity to own that land. He decided to settle in Wisconsin after an American told him that most of the wheat he bought came from that state.

But Daniel knew little of farming. He passed over rich bottomland, choosing a thinly-soiled homestead because it had plenty of wood and water.

John, however, gloried in the magic Wisconsin woods and meadows that "seemed far too marvelous to be real." On the large pond that Daniel named Fountain Lake, water bugs skimmed and played, "dancing to music we could never hear." Nuthatches and bluebirds, chickadees and thrushes chorused from the trees while the boys wondered how woodpeckers "could bore holes so perfectly round." Muir rejoiced: "This sudden plash into pure wilderness — baptism in Nature's warm heart — how utterly happy it made us! ... Here

"I canna get doon," wails young Davie Muir, gripped by fear during a roof-climbing contest. John, clinging precariously to the windowsill, rescued his brother.

without knowing it we still were at school; every wild lesson a love lesson, not whipped but charmed into us. Oh, that glorious Wisconsin wilderness!"

Time has changed Muir's virgin Wisconsin, but the lake — now called Ennis Lake, but referred to as Muir Lake by some people — remains wild and varied. A stroll near its shore took me from a bog of tangled roots and muddy water through wild rushes and grasses to a garden of hip-high wild flowers — and then on to a briar patch, an aspen thicket, an oak grove, and

Slow rhythm of the North Sea still sets the pace of life in Dunbar. At the city harbor, gulls fight for scraps from a fish-cleaner's knife; nearby, youngsters scramble down a retaining wall to a small boat. Young John Muir relished the wildness of the sea, the meadows, the hills, and the headlands near his home on High Street. He would steal out of the family house, which later became the Lorne Temperance Hotel (above), and ramble in the country as often as school and chores would permit. He loved to run to the fields and listen to skylarks or roam along the shore "to gaze and wonder at the shells and seaweeds, eels and crabs . . . in spite of the sure sore punishment that followed like shadows" from his father. One evening, Daniel Muir announced to his children: "Bairns, you needna learn your lessons the nicht, for we're gan to America the morn!"

finally a mini-world of cup fungi and castlelike lichens, all within a mere fifty paces of each other!

"Muir Lake is extremely rich—and distinctive—in plant life," botanist Hugh Iltis told me. Director of the University of Wisconsin Herbarium, Dr. Iltis once collected more than 250 plant species on a brief foray to the lakeshore; soil types vary so widely, he explained, that one patch of ground only a foot higher than another often supports entirely different flora.

Muir himself prized the lake's myriad plant life and in later years sought to preserve it. But eventually the farm was sold; cattle grazed among his beloved orchids and lilies. Happily, the lake now lies within the 160-acre John Muir County Park, a dream of Syl Adrian, who lives in nearby Montello.

Syl's interest in Muir began some 28 years ago, when "I learned that Muir was a high-school dropout and an inventor. Well so am I!" Muir toyed mainly with clocks and pendulums; Syl's past creations include "The X-Ray Shoe-Fitter" and an eight-record jukebox called the Adrianola, with a coin slot that accepts nickels, dimes, or quarters. Similar slots—an Adrian first—today operate virtually every candy and soft-drink machine in the world.

As we talked in Syl's one-room Indian Museum—stuffed with beadwork and weaponry of the Winnebago tribe as well as several Adrian inventions—a visitor slipped a coin into Syl's "Violino Virtuoso," a mechanically played violin and piano combination. The whining, mildly out-of-tune duet lent nostalgic background music to our talk.

"Marquette County was Muir's home," Syl explained. "But he'd never been honored with a single sign or marker." Now, in addition to the county park, the lake and 35 surrounding acres have been designated the Muir Lake Scientific Area, as part of a statewide program to preserve certain tracts of land for their unique botanical value. Muir, I think, would approve.

Amid rushes at the south end of the lake, John learned to swim by imitating frogs. But he rarely found time for such play. "We were all made slaves through the vice of over-industry," he wrote. All, that is, except his father, who in the words of a neighbor "preferred preaching to working." Daniel became known for long prayers and longer sermons—seven days a week. Most of his farm duties fell to eldest son John: "I was put to the plough at the age of twelve, when my head reached but little above the handles. . . . It was hard work for so small a boy. . . ." Muir also became the family rail-splitter, sapling-chopper, and stump-digger, and though proud of these manly skills, he felt such drudgery "stopped my growth and earned for me the title 'Runt of the family.' "

John's 17-hour workday dawned with inescapable routine: "grinding scythes, feeding the animals, chopping stove-wood, and carrying water up the hill from the spring. . . ." Following

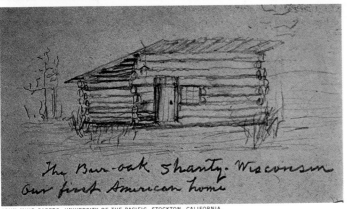

The Bur-oak shanty. Wisconsin
Our first American home

Three generations of the Harry Kearns family stand before their Hickory Hill farmhouse—built in 1857 by the Muir family. John's father, Daniel, moved his wife and children from Scotland in 1849 in search of land for farming. Of their first Wisconsin home—a roughhewn cabin—only John's sketch (left) remains.

a quick breakfast, he spent a full day harvesting or haying, ate supper at dark, did more chores, worshiped, and went to bed.

Through the dog days of summer, John watched as "fat folk grew lean and the lean leaner," while his own cheeks, rosy from Scotland, faded to yellow. "Many of our old neighbors toiled and sweated and grubbed themselves into their graves years before their natural dying days, in getting a living on a quarter-section of land and vaguely trying to get rich, while bread and raiment might have been serenely won on less than a fourth of this land...." Little wonder John grew up believing that living was more important than getting a living.

Yet his chores droned on: "the axe and plough were kept very busy; cattle, horses, sheep, and pigs multiplied; barns and corncribs were filled up...and in a very short time the new country began to look like an old one."

In fact, it *became* old. Daniel Muir, ignorant of soil types and fertilizers, wore out the Fountain Lake farm almost as fast as

Autumn-hued elms shadow North Hall, where John Muir plunged joyously
into the study of science and classics at the University of Wisconsin in
Madison. Muir enrolled in 1860—22 years old, almost penniless, and
"desperately . . . thirsty for knowledge and willing to endure anything to get
it." Maintaining a grueling schedule of daytime jobs and late-night study,
he still found time to contrive ingenious mechanical devices, conduct
chemistry experiments, and collect botanical specimens from Lake Mendota
(right), which borders the campus. In June 1863, Muir left the University
of Wisconsin—bound for the "University of the Wilderness."

he wore out his sons. And so only eight years after buying the land, he bought another tract a few miles away, and the painful tedium of felling trees, breaking sod, and carving a homestead out of virgin wilderness began all over again.

The new farm, named Hickory Hill, lacked surface water, so John sank a well—with only hammer and chisel. Lowered to his labors in a bucket, he almost died from poison gas one day. But his unrelenting father kept him boring through solid sandstone until he struck water—90 feet down!

The Muir well, somewhat deeper, now brings water to Hickory Hill's current owner, Harry Kearns. Its wind-driven pumps were churning full tilt the day I arrived. Harry, 86 years old, recalls a tale from the days after *his* father bought Hickory Hill; one day the middle-aged Muir brothers dropped by to reminisce. Walking to the well, David asked John if he remembered the first time he hauled water for the oxen. "Remember? I'll never forget it—they took 70 buckets!"

The Muir boys learned early to catch their fun when they could, for Daniel permitted them only two holidays a year, July 4 and January 1. On those days, they scarcely knew how to spend their unaccustomed leisure. Often, they climbed nearby Observatory Hill, once thought to be the tallest point in Wisconsin. Here, 70 years ago, a hiker found a gnarled cedar growing out of the cracked granite bedrock with "J. Muir 1856" sharply etched on one limb.

That limb is gone now, and so is the tree. But other cedars rise up, as do leafy oaks and hickories, their shadowy silhouettes rent by shafts of sunlight on the summer day I saw them. A cacophony of chirpings, wheezings, croaks, and cluckings merged into the background music of wind in the leaves. That wind, that sunshiny day, made the Hill a getaway place, an enclave of solitude.

Below the lichen-encrusted granite crest sprawls Fountain Lake country—largely farms now, but still dotted with small marshes and dollops of woods on the rolling Wisconsin hills. Pocket forests harboring partridge and deer make it easy to envision the wilderness of Muir's day.

Daniel Muir, Harry Kearns observes, "built his house like a good Scotsman—right in the center of the farm so his boys wouldn't lose any time going to work." That house, like the well, still remains—though greatly changed from the Muir era by the addition of new rooms, roof, and a full brick exterior, veneered right over the old wood frame. John grumbled that the large home contained but one source of heat—the kitchen stove: "scant space for three or four small sticks, around which in hard zero weather all the family of ten persons shivered, and beneath which in the morning we found our socks and coarse, soggy boots frozen solid."

As chilblains and farm work weighed heavy, the same John

Muir who had bade school a gleeful farewell a few years earlier now began to yearn "for real knowledge." He read between chores, learning more "without a teacher in a few scraps of time than in years in school before my mind was ready." His father tried to censor the books John read, approving only religious and mathematical texts while banning novels as "the spawn of Satan."

Still, John borrowed copies of Shakespeare, Milton, and other poets who would influence his later life. He also read journals of explorers Mungo Park and Alexander von Humboldt. And he developed an early love of machinery, at a time when factories sprouted like weeds along Wisconsin's Fox River. To pursue these interests in spite of farm chores, Muir began rising at 1 a.m., his body remarkably adjusting to only five hours of sleep. The cellar became his early-morning workshop, a place to build things with scraps of wood and iron.

In his hands, bits of corset steel became awls, compasses, and other tools. Rocks served as pendulums and counterweights. "Busy almost to craziness," Muir quickly devised a sawmill, pyrometers, hygrometers, barometers, waterwheels, and clocks. An iron rod from an old wagon box evolved into an ingenious thermometer, so sensitive it detected a person's body heat four feet away.

Today, in that dark and cobwebby room, Harry Kearns's grandchildren sort eggs. Overhead beams that Muir helped hew still grip each other in firm mortise-and-tenon clasp. Even electricity—one bare bulb—fails to dispel the darkness that oozes from walls and floor. Surely it was a cold, uncomfortable workshop for Muir—but it served.

No less uncomfortable was his father's habit of berating the inventions as a waste of time—even though Daniel himself had passed long hours whittling as a youth. One reason for the irony might lie in a tale Harry Kearns told me.

"John Muir once made a funny combination lock out of wood spools and some thin wires. He put it on the barn one day and left. But no one else knew how to open it. When a cloudburst sent the threshers sprinting to the barn, they couldn't get in. Both they and the crop got soaked!"

Muir recalled simply that "the parental thrashing weather was very stormy." But even then John found it impossible to stop whittling and inventing. In 1860, at the age of 22, he decided to show his inventions at a state fair in Madison.

He was a smash hit. Crowds surrounded his exhibits for a view of the "early-rising machine," which tipped a person out of bed at an appointed hour; front pages of local newspapers called him the attraction of the fair. But when news of John's success reached the Muir home, his dour father only wrote to him on the sin of vanity.

Daniel's preaching was unnecessary, for John considered

his inventions "of little importance." His continuing quest for knowledge now propelled him toward the University of Wisconsin: "next, it seemed to me, to the Kingdom of Heaven." Still, his lack of money and formal schooling discouraged him from applying—until he learned that some freshmen lived principally on milk and bread delivered to the dormitory.

Muir made his decision and moved to the campus in Madison. Although tuition then amounted to only $32 a term, added costs of books and laboratory expenses drove him to cut his food allotment to as little as fifty cents a week! Graham crackers and milk became the regular diet of this student too poor to afford even the molasses enjoyed by the Sorghum Club. Eventually he sickened, and Daniel—relaxing his usually strict policy—sent his son $90.

John Muir never majored in a particular subject, preferring courses of his own choice. He sought knowledge, not a degree, and soon became known as "the best chemistry student in the University." His classics professor leaned heavily on metaphors and similes, devices Muir would later use often in his prolific writings. A science professor, Ezra Carr, who had studied under naturalist Louis Agassiz, stressed the importance of nature's laboratory and developing "the seeing eye" to probe the mysteries of the cosmos. Dr. Carr also introduced Muir to glaciology, a science Muir later expanded with his own theories. "I shall not forget the Doctor," Muir wrote much later, "who first laid before me the great book of Nature."

Nor would he forget beautiful Lake Mendota, which borders the university. Mendota prompted countless swims and shore walks in search of thrashers, robins, bluebirds, and bobolinks—"gushing, gurgling, inexhaustible fountains of song...."

Botany intrigued him far less than birds—until a student bursting with newfound knowledge came upon Muir under a locust tree and elaborated on its many similarities to the common pea. That the tall locust and the diminutive pea plant were botanical brothers amazed Muir: "This fine lesson charmed me and sent me flying to the woods and meadows in wild enthusiasm." He became a botanist of almost fanatic degree.

And yet he kept up other courses, as well as his inventing. One "very delicate contrivance" measured "the growth of plants and the action of sunlight." A "loafer's chair" concealed a spring-fired blank pistol, which detonated when the would-be loafer settled back into the seat. Terrified, the victim would leap from the chair.

Such curiosities made Muir's North Hall dormitory something of an attraction on campus. A friend reminisced 70 years later on the "early-rising machine": "He entertained us by putting us on the bed, and setting the clock so that in a minute or two we were thrown off."

This and other accounts made me eager to experience

Muir's wonderful contraptions myself. Unfortunately, only sketches remain. The exception is his eye-catching scholar's desk, painstakingly carved from wood, and today preserved at the State Historical Society of Wisconsin in Madison. It resembles an oversize highchair. A ruler and two giant compasses form the front legs; whittled "bookstacks" comprise the rear, each "volume" bearing a detailed spine and binding. Intricately carved hands point out the minute and hour, and the day of the week. More than 15 handmade wood cogs—ranging in diameter from less than an inch to more than two feet—provided both decoration and, unbelievably, motion.

Far from being a passive stick of furniture, this clock-driven desk—activated at a time preset by Muir—picked up a text, opened it to a desired page for a desired interval of time, then returned it to a rack and selected the next book for the reader! This apparatus fascinated me—and all the more because it was envisioned, designed, whittled, and assembled by a mere backwoods boy.

"No, it doesn't work now," Dave McNamara of the Historical Society told me with a sad shake of his head. He explained that visitors had rifled it for souvenirs years ago when the invention was on open display. Replacements from a Muir box of spare parts failed to make it operate again. Now it stands alone, protected by a glass case.

All other Muir creations have disappeared, including the early-riser that served him as an alarm clock. It worked well, because its noise drew complaints from Muir's dormmates. He then asked a janitor to wake him each morning by pulling a cord hung from his window and tied to his toe. One day, a prankster vigorously jerked the cord and nearly hauled Muir out the window!

MUIR HIMSELF was no less entertaining or celebrated than his machines. A friend once vouched, "During twenty years or more of public life, I do not recall a single person that could compare with John Muir as a conversationalist." His confidence and penetrating, glacial-blue eyes commanded the attention of any audience, just as his rusticity attracted one. Muir's mass of hair made him seem "wild as a loon" to his sisters. His beard grew so snarled that one student whimsically suggested that he "set fire to it." Despite such advice, Muir kept his whiskers throughout his life, a wild trademark of this man so in love with wilderness.

Even today, 99-year-old Maude Wells of Portage, Wisconsin, vividly remembers from her childhood several occasions when Muir dined with her father. "That beard was so large and thick" she recalls with a smile, "that when Muir ate, food would get tangled in it and just hang there while he talked. Father was always after him to clean it."

Muir, apparently, was too busy. Shortly after he matriculated, the Civil War began. Many students enlisted in a flush of idealistic patriotism. Others, like Muir, remained in class and —just as idealistically—denounced the evils of war.

Traditionally, the years of college have been a time of discovery, doubt, and concern for the future. These same swirling thoughts that have always weighed on students also beleaguered Muir. One day, pensively contemplating Lake Mendota from his window, he mused, "generation follows generation. We are passing away. How great the need for energy to spend our little while to purpose." Muir wanted to learn, but felt strapped in a world of restrictions. He put off the choice of a major subject of study during his sophomore year. And a year after that, he put off the whole university.

From a hilltop near his beloved Lake Mendota, "with streaming eyes I bade my Alma Mater farewell," a college dropout at 25. Muir had no way of knowing, of course, that 34 years later he would receive an honorary degree, Doctor of Laws, from the University of Wisconsin. He only knew that his once-boundless enthusiasm for a college education had evaporated. Like many students today, he had tired of books: "they are but piles of stones."

After an extended botanizing journey into Canada, Muir again turned to inventing. He found work in an Indianapolis carriage shop, designing machines that increased production of hubs and spokes. Although the job meant leaving nature for the "rush and roar and whirl of the factory," he was successful; his employers thought that in a few years he could even manage his own shop.

One day, Muir was preparing to adjust the drive belt of a machine. While unlacing the belt with the naillike end of a file, it slipped and jabbed deep into his eye. He watched, terror-stricken, as the ocular fluid drained into his cupped hand and the sight of his right eye gradually failed.

"My right eye is gone!" he gasped, "closed forever on all God's beauty!" Muir's anguish later deepened when his good eye also failed. His mind reeled. He would have to give up inventing, botanizing, everything!

He was blind!

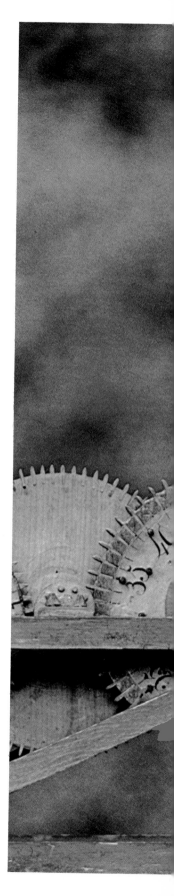

Cogs and dials of polished wood form the clock mechanism of Muir's scholar's desk—an elaborate device that selected a textbook, opened it, then closed it after a specified time. Muir's love for inventing abruptly ended in 1866, when a workshop accident left him temporarily blind.

2

THE THOUSAND-MILE WALK

"Immense swamps . . . completely fenced and darkened, that are never ruffled with winds or scorched with drought": The Okefenokee Swamp matches Muir's impressions of Georgia's river country, which he explored during his walk to the Gulf of Mexico in 1867. Swept downstream while fording the Chattahoochee River in Georgia, Muir (above) grabs overhanging vines to pull himself up the steep embankment.

ENDLESS NIGHTMARES AND DESPAIR consumed the sightless John Muir. "My days were terrible beyond what I can tell, and my nights were if possible more terrible." Thoughts of a wasted life tormented him; his only shred of relief came with joyous memories of the midwestern wilds he had roamed "happy and free, poor and rich . . . independent alike of roads and people." He pondered his dual loves—inventing and "the inventions of God"—and reached a pivotal decision: He would devote himself totally to nature. In the wilderness he had always sensed "a plain, simple relationship to the Cosmos." Now, he longed more than ever to see it.

His doctor had predicted permanent blindness. But during four weeks of convalescence in a darkened room, vision slowly returned to both eyes. "Now had I arisen from the grave!" Muir exclaimed. "God has nearly to kill us sometimes, to teach us lessons." True to his vow, he shunned the world of factories—although his former employers promised him a raise and an eventual partnership. "I might have become a millionaire," he fondly recalled later, "but I chose to become a tramp!"

Muir's tramping would become global in scale. Since boyhood, explorer Alexander von Humboldt's journals had intrigued him with reports of South American mysteries. Now, prodded even more by his love of botany, Muir's mind was set, "How intensely I desire to be a Humboldt!" He would sail to South America, explore Venezuela's Orinoco River and then raft down the Amazon through Brazil to the Atlantic. To prepare himself both botanically and physically for the tropics, he first would take a shakedown walk through the southern states, hiking the thousand miles from Louisville, Kentucky, to the Gulf of Mexico.

Such ambitions showed an astonishing lack of planning. Only two days before leaving for Louisville, Muir wrote, "I wish I knew where I was going." When family and friends asked his proposed route, he simply shrugged his shoulders and said, "Oh! I don't know—just anywhere in the wilderness." And then he was gone, "with a plant-press on my back, holding a generally southward course, like the birds when they are going from summer to winter." The year was 1867, his age 29.

One hundred and eight years later, I set off in my 29th year with plant press and free heart to retrace that odyssey. Muir had chosen Louisville because it was the historic gateway to the South. But his walk actually began in neighboring Jeffersonville, Indiana, end of the line for his southbound train. There, he spent the night. Next morning, he crossed the brown, churning waters of the Ohio River and entered Louisville, steering through the city "without speaking a word to any one." His journal, published much later as *A Thousand-Mile Walk to the Gulf*, often expounds a marked distaste for anything urban. "Escaped to the woods," he wrote. Later he added: "I escaped to the fields...." "Escaped ... to the generous bosom of the woods," reads another entry.

Muir became a lifelong escapist, fleeing city grime for the "wildest, leafiest, and least trodden way" through the land. Except for his need of food, wrote Muir, "I doubt if civilization would ever see me again." Outside Louisville, great wild oaks "spread their arms in welcome," making Kentucky an "Eden, the paradise of oaks."

His words still apply. I was surprised by Kentucky's spreading forests of oaks and other hardwoods—surprised that they exist at all in a land that has known the bite of ax and plow for more than two centuries. Often, the very texture of the land makes it seem old: Surface shale on its slump-shouldered hills crumbles underfoot, as if too timeworn to withstand the strain. But the trees, the bluegrass, and the wild flowers soften such age lines with a green freshness that is perpetually renewed.

My first night in Kentucky, I camped in the style of John Muir—without food or proper equipment. I had no stove, no flashlight, no knife, no compass, no tent or ground cloth. My sole concession to the 20th century was a sleeping bag; I pitched camp by tossing it on the ground and crawling inside.

I lay in Muir's "one great bedroom of the night." A crescent moon limned the oak boughs overhead; stars blossomed and *moved*—no, they were only lightning bugs. Frogs, crickets, whippoorwills, and other creatures chanted their tireless nocturne. Strangely, my bumpy bed didn't bother me. I felt a primeval peace, a contentment, a feeling that man—even modern man—is somehow at home among leaves and the clean, damp smell of the woods. I slept.

Several hours later, a brilliant yellow-white flash crowded the dome of my mind, jolting me awake. There was another flash, and yet another—lightning! Whole sectors of light invaded the sky. The bursts grew nearer, rousing their namesake lightning bugs to new heights of activity, until falling rain chased the insects into hiding.

Muir would have loved it. He was the sort who knew enough *not* to come in out of the rain. His passion for raw nature drove him to weather storms from unprotected hilltops and trees, vantage points where his mind might soar with the raging "love-beats of Nature's heart."

My mind enjoys the beauty of lightning as much as anyone's. But that night it could not blot out the incessant complaints from my body: cold, wet, uncomfortable.

Happily, the rain soon tapered off, and I again fell asleep. A sunless dawn caught runnels of fog silently probing the valleys below me as I set off, Muir-like, among the trees. Whenever I brushed a branch or grabbed out for support, big, cold drops showered me. I was totally soaked in two minutes. But wetness brought its own reward—freedom. I remembered once as a child hopping on stepping-stones across a stream and being meticulously careful to avoid the water—until a shoe-drenching misstep liberated me. I couldn't get any wetter, so I plunged ahead, throwing myself completely into that new watery world. So it was in the woods.

I ran, dodging trees and underbrush, racing without competition, space, or time. I was locked in dense forest, a skyless realm where black and green were the only colors, and wetness was the only sensation. Every bit of space not taken by inky tree trunks was jammed with the green of new spring leaves, a green so delicate and soft it seemed to be the very atmosphere itself. A deer, spooked by my twig-snapping charge, whuffed and bounded off. But the green formed a barrier so impervious that I never saw the deer, any more than I could see the pileated woodpecker that called, somewhere, above me.

Below this green wilderness, Muir wandered through a wilderness of grays—the subterranean domes, boulevards, and mazy side streets of Mammoth Cave in south central Kentucky. He was "surprised to find it in so complete naturalness." Each year, more than half a million similarly surprised visitors marvel at this underground national park. Mammoth is but one of more than 100 caves pitting the area. Some are padlocked—not to keep bizarre creatures in, but to keep human intruders out.

Gary Talley, a Park technician, took me into one such locked cave. Its heavy door creaked open slowly; drops of water plunked and plashed somewhere in the darkness. Hundreds of strange-looking "camelback crickets"—long-legged, completely white insects—skittered in the glare of Gary's lantern. Thumb-size bats clung to the ceiling only inches from my head. I did not feel comfortable.

But beyond the entrance, all fears evaporated in the glow of the cave's startling beauty. We could have been in King Solomon's mines. Millions of sparkling crystals—more numerous than stars on the darkest night—shot back the lantern's blaze. We were surrounded by an underground galaxy of gleaming, twinkling gypsum—crystals of calcium sulphate fashioned into extraordinary shapes. Gemlike obelisks reached up from the floor; thin "soda straws" and helical "wood shavings" hung from above; translucent sheets gleamed like mica; hairlike needles resembled fine white fur. The show was endless. Like Muir, I rejoiced "to find so much music in stony silence, so much splendor in darkness."

Ahead, a serpentine passageway of hip-scraping dimensions led to a chamber of hanging gardens. Gypsum rosettes and vines and blossoms—many larger than magnolias and just as exquisite—flourished here, formed by gradual buildup of the white mineral. I wondered aloud how rock could be so delicate, so flowerlike.

"No one really knows why gypsum takes so many different

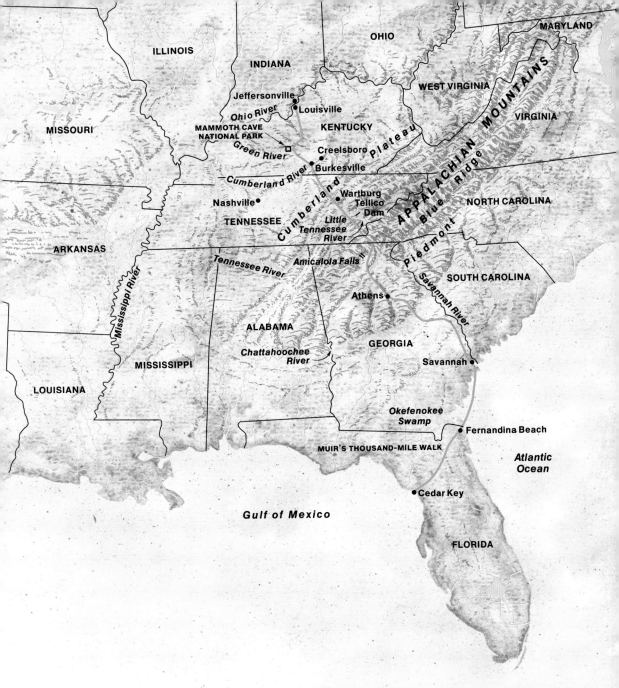

On his first long botanical walk, John Muir spanned the
southeastern United States. For years, he had longed to
see the "tropic gardens" at the "warm end of the
country." Muir planned his journey a few miles south of
Louisville, Kentucky: "I spread out my map under a
tree and made up my mind to go through Kentucky,
Tennessee, and Georgia to Florida, thence to Cuba,
thence to some part of South America; but it will be only
a hasty walk." In less than two months, he covered
some one thousand miles to Cedar Key, Florida.

shapes," Gary answered. "But one thing's for sure—it can't take water." Unlike real flowers, gypsum can dissolve; a mere change in humidity can blur petals and leaves. Only the cave's incredibly static conditions enable such fragile creations to survive for centuries.

But then they have to. A single tulip-size bloom takes several thousand years to form, Gary told me. "Makes you feel pretty insignificant," he added quietly. I could only agree as I stared at a ten-inch-long hank of gypsum "rope," unable to believe that this delicate stony outpouring had begun to form long before the first pharaoh ruled Egypt.

I thought it unfortunate that only bats and crickets regularly inhabit this ancient wilderness. But gypsum fares poorly in man's presence, and so the door stays locked.

Dual forces of solution and erosion carved Kentucky's ornate caves out of solid limestone, sometimes so completely that the roofs have collapsed, triggering surface depressions called "sinks." Gary's father-in-law almost lost a tractor when a sink suddenly formed beneath him. Cedar Sink, one of 10,000 such pockmarks in central Kentucky, stretches a quarter of a mile wide and 200 feet deep. Rich soil lining the bottom of this pit once made it preferred farmland. Today, it is a steep-walled jungle of cedars, oaks, redbuds, and dogwoods. Despite all the handholds these trees afforded, we slipped and slid for the entire 200 feet down. I asked Gary how the farmers had hauled their crops out of mud-slick Cedar Sink.

"Maybe all the corn they grew didn't leave as grain," he answered with a wink. In these parts of the Appalachians, I later learned, some farmers have always shown a preference for the more compact, liquid form of corn.

Muir never mentioned "white lightning" and backwoods stills; he focused his attention primarily on caves, trees, and mountain peaks—the first he had seen. A lifelong love affair with mountains began south of cave country, in the corrugated Cumberland Plateau, western spur of the Appalachian Mountains. Like the fingers of some gigantic green hand, these forested ridgelines parallel each other in a southwesterly slant from eastern Kentucky through Tennessee. I knew I was in Tennessee only when the state's Stars and Bars joined the Stars and Stripes on the post-office flagpole.

Muir's 1867 trek began just two years after the end of the Civil War, a harrowing time to travel the mountains unarmed and without friends. Everywhere he saw desperate poverty in a land prostrated by war. Some people, stripped of farms and jobs, turned to thievery, waylaying whoever dared to pass through the area. Yet Muir ventured here alone, afoot, and unafraid—and probably so obviously impoverished that few highwaymen would waste time holding him up. One who did, found in Muir's bag "only a comb, brush, towel, soap, a change of underclothing, a copy of Burns's poems, Milton's *Paradise Lost*, and a small New Testament." The robber returned the bag.

Alone again, Muir gladly continued, finding utter wildness and joy in the steep Plateau. He soon learned that its rivers formed the best trails, and he followed them as much for guidance as for beauty. A favorite of Muir's was the Cumberland River, a narrow stream that constantly doubles back on itself, speaking in laughing, splashing tones.

Near Burkesville, in southern Kentucky, I watched the evening mists veneer the Cumberland. Swallows flitted between the green banks, skimming the water for a drink. I recalled Muir's words, "The Cumberland must be a happy stream." Sundown came, and with it, peace.

Heading upstream the next day, I traced the river past Creelsboro to its abrupt end. Here, Wolf Creek Dam plugs the Cumberland River, making a 64,000-acre lake that fills power and recreation needs. But in so doing, it has drowned the Cumberland hillsides. Gone is the floodplain-to-ridgeline mystique of a winding river valley of farms and ravines and forest. Only lake and hilltops remain. I stood on the dam, able to see both Muir's Cumberland and the modern one, and I wondered how happy his river is today.

Dams and man-made lakes are sprinkled throughout the Cumberland Plateau. Many have been built by the Tennessee Valley Authority over the last few decades to provide power and flood control; these dam projects also brought much-needed employment. "Because these benefits were so badly needed," Tennessean Bob Brandt told me, "for years saying anything against TVA was like spitting on grandmother's grave. But now things have changed." He told me of a current controversy — the Tellico Dam under construction on the Little Tennessee River. "One of the finest trout streams in the eastern U. S. — and they're going to dam it. And it won't even have a power plant!"

Why, I asked, in this era of nationwide energy crisis, would anyone build a powerless dam?

"They say it's for economic development and recreational use," he answered. But the dam will displace 300 farming families and flood ancient Cherokee Indian sites. "Because of all these reasons," Brandt said, "a lot of people around here are against Tellico." A Nashville attorney and conservationist, Brandt was "raised up" in east Tennessee, where an outdoor life helped develop an early appreciation for his native land. He doesn't want it despoiled.

Brandt told me that while TVA still concentrates most of its budget on power production, only 13 percent of that power is hydroelectric. "Almost all the rest is coal-fired — so TVA's all for strip mining." TVA owns some 130,000 acres of east Tennessee coal country, much of it "steep as a horse's face." Steep land aggravates the drawbacks (Continued on page 57)

Cloaked in mist, the Cumberland River flows through gently rolling hills near Burkesville, Kentucky. Muir described it as "a happy stream. I think I could enjoy traveling with it in the midst of such beauty all my life." Plumes of flowering beard-grass (opposite, top) ripple in a soft breeze on the Cumberland Plateau. Indian grass (opposite, bottom) thrives on dry mountain slopes. Muir admired the shapes, growing habits, and "wind-waving gestures" of grasses. "But all of them are beautiful beyond the reach of language. I rejoice that God has 'so clothed the grass of the field.'"

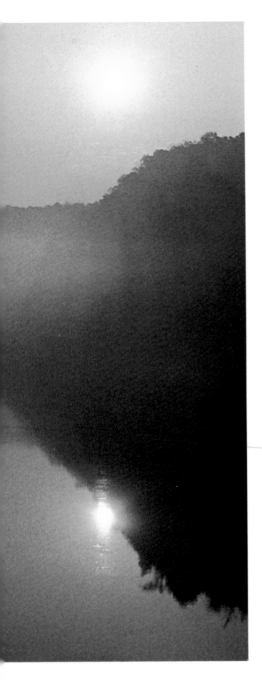

"...I spent some joyous time in a grand rock-dwelling full of mosses, birds, and flowers."

Massive brow of Moore Rock overhangs two
visitors in Frozen Head State Park near
Wartburg, Tennessee. John Muir took shelter in
such a "rock-dwelling" as he traveled south
across the Cumberland Plateau; "Most heavenly
place I ever entered," he rhapsodized. Above,
Tennessee farmer Louis Jones drives his mule
team as it hauls a homemade wooden sled
through a creek and up its steep bank. "More
reliable than a tractor any day," he maintains.
Muir encountered many such backwoods farmers, who shared with him their hard-earned
food, roughhewn houses, and colorful stories.

"...fogs...are grand, far-reaching affairs..."

Rivers of fog drift through valleys of the Blue Ridge in Georgia. Muir reached the "last mountain summit" in September; before him stretched a "uniform expanse of dark pine woods, extending to the sea. . . ."

of strip mines, which produce coal in the quickest way. The mines also produce eyesores in the Tennessee landscape. Brandt explained: Stripping exposes deadly iron pyrite, source of acid that dooms the soil, muddies streams, and kills fish. A 1972 Tennessee law directs mining companies to bury all black, acid-producing material. I discovered that most mine owners— including TVA—are making efforts to return the land to productivity. But the struggle is difficult, and proper reclamation methods are still being tested.

Tennessee conservationist Don Todd showed me one reclaimed strip mine atop a leveled-off mountain. It had been smoothed, fertilized, and sown with four tons of lime per acre in an attempt to neutralize the acid and comply with the law.

Unfortunately, this attempt failed. Acid-generating pyrite still held sway, as evidenced by frail, brown scatterings of grass over the shaly "soil"—black as if burned. Four-inch pine seedlings planted only a few months earlier had withered.

"Some didn't last more than two weeks," said Don, as we walked over a devastated and barren land. Runoff gullies channeled the earth, burgeoning with each rain into muddy cascades that tear loose vegetation.

Such effects of stripping cannot be ignored. Even at a distance of five miles, gray slashes of runoff and landslides leap out from otherwise verdant peaks. Huge concentric gouges spiral up Big Brushy Mountain, peeling it like a huge apple. For me, such visual scars in the land recalled lines from a song about a Kentucky county just west of Muir's ramblings:

'Daddy, won't you take me back to Muhlenberg County,
Down by the Green River where Paradise lay?'
'Sorry my son, but you're too late in asking—
Mister Peabody's coal train has hauled it away.'

The Peabody that the songwriter refers to is a giant coal company, western Kentucky's major employer and money-maker. Although Peabody never mined coal in the town of Paradise, the verse alludes to an awareness of the problems of strip mining.

Despite its shortcomings, stripping continues with few local outcries. One reason, Don suggests, is a strong sense of ownership rights in these mountains.

Economics also deter Tennesseans—coal means money and jobs, no matter how it's taken from the earth. And traditionally, residents always considered land something to use, to cut over and mine and farm and settle—and then move on.

"And why not?" Don asked. "The mountains seemed endless—if you stripped one there'd always be more behind it."

In many ways, Tennessee's streams, forests, and valleys still seem endless today. But no land is inexhaustible. Muir preached this long before most of his contemporaries did; he

Splashing and swirling over water-worn rocks, Amicalola Falls in northern Georgia spills 729 feet down a precipice. On a similar autumn day in 1867, John Muir stood at the summit of a commanding ridge nearby and "obtained a magnificent view of blue, softly curved mountain scenery." Amicalola Falls takes its lilting name from the Cherokee Indian word for "tumbling waters."

criticized unbridled industry in the South as "The gobble gobble school of economics." Bob Brandt, Don Todd, and other local citizens sympathize. "We're just beginning to realize we've almost used up our scenic resources," Don said. And so 110 years after the Civil War, a war of another sort rages across the Cumberland Plateau—one of dams and mining, clear-cutting and environment.

I find the Plateau itself to be something of a puzzle. Rich green tracts of wilderness and farm make it a land of plenty, yet the area traditionally has been economically poor. This, I discovered, is because outsiders have removed and gained the profit from much of its wealth—crops, cattle, timber, coal.

There's something wrong, I thought one day as I bored into a local restaurant's meal of green beans and fried okra. The beans came straight from a can and the okra was more fry than okra. And I had seen fresh produce harvested from local farms that very morning.

Indeed, farming was once the region's mainstay, the magnet that long ago convinced independent-minded men to leave the developed East Coast and become mountaineers. Men like Louis Jones of Wartburg, Tennessee.

Louis is a mountain man, a lifelong bachelor, a God-fearing, honest, country sort who gets up before the sun to work his 120 acres and who always wears out the knees of his overalls before the seat. He's friendly and hospitable, glad to share what he can with a stranger. He's the kind of man Muir often relied on for food during his walk.

Uncounted days in the sun have burned Louis's arms, face, and neck the same red-brown as his long-farmed soil. "I'll be 62 next week, and I haven't been away from here for one whole day since 1938!" His voluntary confinement hasn't hurt him; his brown eyes still chuckle warmly, his body is hard, his teeth remain sparkling.

Shunning a tractor, Louis farms with two mules: "Find I can get around a lot easier. Might want to haul a single log out of the woods—with a tractor, I'd have to cut a road through first. With mules, it's no trouble."

And instead of a wheeled wagon, he relies on a sturdy, homemade wooden sled about a foot high. "Sleds don't last too long, but they sure are the handiest thing—see, you don't have to lift things way up high, like with a cart. You just drop on your load and go." Louis hitched his team of mules to the sled with tattered, patched harnesses and took off with 500 pounds of fertilizer—and 205 pounds of me—in tow. His sled handled every terrain that we encountered, sliding through grass, rocky fields, and creeks with equal ease.

I marveled at how the mules responded to voice commands, then stood patiently in the hot sun as their owner left to sow the fertilizer by hand, like seed. They didn't even mind his dawdling here and there to hunt arrowheads, one of Jones's favorite hobbies.

Later we passed Louis's roadside gate—tied open in a gesture of hospitality—and came to his long, low cabin of square logs, dovetailed and sheathed with boards. A swing graced the broad porch, shaded by three old maples. Its view takes in the valley and mountains beyond.

We entered the cabin, and Louis sat on an oak chair as aged as his century-old home. His heels have worn valleys in the chair's cross brace, but it hasn't weakened. "My daddy always told me old virgin timber would outlast anything—and *his* daddy told him." Louis then showed me an old square maple tray whittled, not by his grandfather, but by his grandfather's grandfather! Its maker used it for mixing corn bread; so does Louis. Despite its nearly 150 years of hard use, I couldn't find a single crack in that tray.

The brawny virgin trees that produced the wood for such marvelous trays no longer cover the land, of course. But Louis owns a few giants, 500-year-old oaks, sycamores, and scaly-bark hickories that grow more than four feet wide at chest height. They are so big, so tall, that I could not see individual leaves. Nor could Louis, who knows each species by its bark and the appearance of its trunk. Wild grapevines drape some trees with eight-inch-thick coils.

Louis's home suits its rustic surroundings. It lacks plumbing—a clean "branch" flows past the house—but it has electricity: Louis appreciates a bit of light after dawn-to-dusk labors.

I glanced about his kitchen and noticed a mass of spider webs shrouding the corners of this otherwise clean room. Louis's eyes followed mine, and he smiled. "You don't see a fly now, do you? Old-time housekeepers would just about kill you if you took down their spider webs."

Meals in Louis's home are simple and usually homegrown. "You know, I can make a full meal out of peanuts—just roast them up and have some corn bread—it's great." He then stoked up the wood stove for dinner and went out with a pail for water, whistling joyously. The kitchen table soon sagged under country-size servings of corn bread and beans.

"Hang on and I'll get some milk," he added, pulling a big pitcher—frosted with a thick yellow crust of hardened cream—from the refrigerator.

I've never been a great lover of milk, and that crust made me doubtful about becoming one—especially after Louis stirred it up and poured me a glass full of floating yellow chunks. Against my better judgment, but unwilling to brand myself an incurable city boy, I downed some of that strange liquid.

Elixir! It was the best, sweetest, tastiest milk I can ever recall. It had come straight from cow to table, unpasteurized, unhomogenized, untouched. Yet despite its flavor, Louis "can't sell it—can't even give it away. It's the law, see. Milk's gotta be pasteurized." And so he throws out three-fourths of the milk his cow produces, keeping only enough for himself.

Louis once kept "a couple hundred" chickens as well. "Used to peddle milk, eggs, butter. But you can't sell anymore —too many laws against the small man. Today, I'm just ground-hogging it"—raising enough only for his own needs. His cash crop, sweet corn, pays for the store-bought supplies he gets every three weeks: "Ten pounds of flour, some sugar, cornmeal, oatmeal, maybe a pound of bacon." Louis's profits enable him to live "just the way I like," he said with a contented grin, as the sound of boiling water signaled dishwashing time.

Louis is something of an anachronism—even in the old hills of Tennessee. Too proud and too much in love with his land to sell off timber or mineral rights, he clings to farming. When he needs something, he always looks first to himself. "There's very, very few full-time farmers today. Can't pay help more than a dollar an hour or you're in the hole. I've seen a lot of people try to farm here and have to leave." Yet Louis remains, a model of determination. He seemed more than a little like John Muir when he added, "The mountains are my life. Never been away from them very long; don't feel quite right when I am away. People from here always come back."

As I left Louis, the bright moon revealed mists filling the valley beneath those silhouetted mountains. The scene was quiet, serene, beautiful. I understood his affection for the land.

Muir felt a similar bond to the Tennessee mountains. But the call of Humboldt drew him ever southward, through north-ern Georgia's foothills to the totally unwild city of Athens—so named because the University of Georgia made it a center of learning and culture, reminiscent of its namesake in Greece.

"The most beautiful town I have seen on the journey," Muir wrote. Unlike other cities he had visited—and immediately shunned—this one lured him to stay and explore. Classic man-sions of wealthy planters abounded with antebellum grace even though Muir arrived after the Civil War; Athens lay outside the scourge of Sherman's march to the sea.

Ironically, the decades since Muir's visit have been less kind than the war years. "Dozens of old homes were torn down because of Athens' expansion, both in the commercial district and at the university," Mrs. Homer C. Cooper of the Athens His-torical Society told me. "I'm so thankful that sororities and fra-ternities have bought many of the places and saved them."

Though its bloom may have faded, antebellum Athens is no dying flower. Take a stroll down Dearing Street, where old middle-class homes—formerly one to each four-acre city block

—sprout Italianate arches or Creole ironwork. The real mansions, spaciously accommodated on six or eight acres, display even more elegance: massive Corinthian columns, verandas, spiral steps, and flowering magnolias—all bathed in the musky odor of formal boxwood hedges that maze the front garden. Echoes abound of pre-Civil War prosperity and hospitality.

Such elegance, however, detained Muir for only a day. His lust for nature drove him on—at a fast pace of 25 miles a day—to the undulating foothills of the Piedmont, which in turn tumble into Georgia's flat coastal plain. There, planters had staked their lives and fortunes on cotton. Yet much land remained unfarmed, and it captured Muir's attention. "Grasses are becoming tall and cane-like and do not cover the ground with their leaves as at the North," he recorded. Soon came the magic of Georgia's swamps, filled with "remarkable" cypresses: "... the only level-topped tree that I have seen. The branches, though spreading, are careful not to pass each other, and stop suddenly on reaching the general level, as if they had grown up against a ceiling." (Continued on page 67)

Pausing on a grassy knoll in Kentucky, John Muir reflects: "Another day in the most favored province of bird and flower.... The soft light of morning falls upon ripening forests ... and all Nature is thoughtful and calm." Throughout his long walk to the Gulf, Muir recorded his thoughts in a rambling journal and preserved hundreds of botanical specimens in the plant press at his side.

Stately survivor of pre-Civil War days, the Grant-Hill
Mansion in Athens, Georgia, houses the president of
the University of Georgia. Muir described Athens as
"a remarkably beautiful and aristocratic town, con-
taining many classic and magnificent mansions. . . ."
Scratching his chin with work-worn hands, 91-year-
old "Uncle George" Scott reminisces about life on
the Wade Plantation north of Savannah. "All cotton,
cotton, nothin' but cotton. Yes, sir, whooee! Had an
oil mill, too, to make oil from the seeds."

Silvery swags of Spanish moss festoon live oak and magnolia trees in
Savannah's Bonaventure Cemetery. While awaiting a money packet
mailed by his brother, Muir took refuge for nearly a week from thieves
and vandals in this "weird and beautiful abode of the dead." On the
first night he slept beneath a spreading oak tree (above, top). "I found a
little mound that served for a pillow, placed my plant press and bag
beside me and rested fairly well...." Muir wrote lyrical descriptions
of the cemetery's abundant plant and animal life, including insects
such as the grasshopper clinging to the petal of a rain lily (above).

Cypress swamps inundate parts of the state even today, largely along the great brown swath of the Savannah River. Muir, apparently unconcerned about snakes or alligators, tramped alone. I chose instead to rely on a "swamp fox," native Georgian Karus Kittles.

Karus is the son of former slaves. His face carries an intricate, intriguing network of wrinkles; even Karus isn't sure when he was born. He is probably well into his eighties. "Can't read nor write. Can't do figures neither." But dates and ages and the three R's mean little in his timeless homeland, where life still depends heavily on common sense and backcountry know-how. Karus is strong in both.

My first swamp lesson began with Karus pointing out deer tracks, a raccoon's "handprints," and the trail of a wildcat. Then he began beating the brush carefully.

"Know what I'm hunting? That there." He proudly held up a three-inch-high stalk. "Coonroot!" he grinned. To Karus, it was medicine. "Put it in gin and drink it and it'll fix you right up—don't have to worry none about age." This mysterious restorative, I slowly deciphered from Karus's knowing looks and smiles, would fend off impotence, just as sure as brierberry root would cure "bad blood." Karus harvests many such wild medicines—both for himself and for others. It has been part of his outdoor life for decades.

"Been fishing and hunting all my days. There's deer and ducks here; catfish, bass, mudfish, too." Local populations of raccoon, alligator, and wild hog helped his family—"eleven head of children"—survive the Depression, a time Karus knows only as "Hoover Days." It was a time when he was glad to work the fields for 40 cents a day.

"Used to see droves of wild hogs—25 or 30 at a time," he told me as we walked slowly down a dirt backroad. "Used to be a lot of turkey too. But now, hogs all hunted out. Don't see no more turkey, neither."

Just then I spotted a wild turkey—right in the middle of the road. Later, Karus promised we'd turn up plenty of rattlesnakes. We didn't see one. I began to doubt my guide.

Further doubts would follow. In a ten-foot boat, we explored swamplands that lay in overwhelming stillness. Not a wisp of wind rippled the waters, stained a murky purplish-brown by decaying leaves and bark. An occasional birdcall or the lonely plop of a jumping fish reverberated in the silence of this natural echo chamber. Towering cypress trees—densely hung with foliage and netlike Spanish moss—rimmed each motionless pool like giant beaded curtains as we slowly paddled through the watery labyrinth.

Whenever I looked back to try to fix our direction, the trees seemed identical to the scene before us—or to the left or right. I felt a quick surge of panic. We could easily get lost in this

Motionless water mirrors a great egret on Sea Island off Georgia's coast. Muir traveled by steamship from Savannah to Fernandina Beach, Florida, to avoid "an unwalkable piece of forest," the Okefenokee Swamp. "For a few hours our steamer sailed in the open sea ... but most of the time she threaded her way among the lagoons, the home of alligators and countless ducks and waders."

trackless wilderness. I pestered my guide for reassurances.

"I know every stick in the woods," Karus replied. My doubts began to subside. "But on water, I don't know *where* I am."

I was shattered. So he doesn't know any more about swamps than he does about wild turkeys! Every direction seemed wrong; nothing looked familiar except what lay behind. But it's no use, I thought, *I* can't lead us out of here. It's up to Karus.

He succeeded—and in short order. Apparently, as a joke, he'd made a circle trip, rather than retrace our wake, and just let the city slicker sweat out being "lost" for a time.

WHILE IN THESE SWAMPS, Muir contemplated floating down the Savannah River. But feet, not a raft, took him to the port city of Savannah.

Too poor to afford the meanest Savannah hotel for more than one night, he set up camp in Bonaventure Cemetery as he waited for a prearranged packet of money to arrive from his brother. Here, Muir thought, he would at least be safe from thieves and marauders. For a week he slept on a Spanish-moss bed, beneath a roof of rushes, drinking stagnant, muddy water, eating crackers—and rejoicing. To him, the graveyard seemed "so beautiful that almost any sensible person would choose to dwell here with the dead rather than with the lazy, disorderly living." Bald eagles nested in the live oaks. Warblers and butterflies cheered him without end, making Bonaventure "a center of life. The dead do not reign there alone."

More a wild park than close-cropped cemetery, Bonaventure remains delightfully untrimmed. I arrived just after a rainstorm had left it glistening. The sun, filtering through leafy oaks, dappled grounds scattered with shiny magnolia leaves. A quail's rustling stutter broke the silence; breezes brought forth the clean smell of salt marsh. Azaleas, camellias, roses, and wisteria blossomed in unpruned abandon. All wore tangled crowns of Spanish moss, so prolific that concerned citizens once staged a cleanup day for Bonaventure, and stripped the offending growth from the shrubbery.

"It was fine for a few months," recalls Sam Monk, director of the Savannah Park and Tree Commission, which then had jurisdiction over the cemetery. "But the moss came right back. The moss-pickers seemed to realize it was a losing cause—they haven't ever tried again."

I *like* the droopy, ubiquitous Spanish moss. I like its feeling of peace, the way it sways with every breeze, the way it screens the hot Georgia sun. I also like the way Bonaventure's moss-draped oaks merge in grand cathedral arches that—as much as any headstones—make visitors feel that here is consecrated ground. Nature has consecrated it.

Yet despite this aura of wildness, Bonaventure owes its beauty largely to one man's careful plans. Colonel John Mulryne planted the live oaks some 200 years ago to complement what was perhaps the finest 18th-century home in Savannah. A doubtful but persistent tale holds that when Mulryne's house caught fire during a dinner party, the gracious host—unwilling to let the festivities collapse—ordered tables and chairs moved outdoors among the oaks, where his guests dined in the glare of the flames. The story does not recount what they did for light after the home had burned to the ground—or where Mulryne slept that night.

Bonaventure's plentiful palmettos, spirea, and other plants made it a ready laboratory for botanist Muir, who found in it "one of the most impressive assemblages of animal and plant creatures." Among the animals, mosquitoes, flies, and "prickly-footed beetles" harassed Muir throughout his stay. Yet he was happy, intrigued by nature's hold on the cemetery. "She corrodes the iron and marble, and gradually levels the hill which is always heaped up, as if a sufficiently heavy quantity of clods could not be laid on the dead. Arching grasses come one by one; seeds come flying on downy wings. . . . Life at work everywhere, obliterating all memory of the confusion of man." Muir's conclusion: "death is stingless indeed, and as beautiful as life. . . . All is divine harmony."

When at last his money arrived, Muir bought a steamer ticket to Fernandina Beach, in northeast Florida, enabling him to bypass "a very sickly, entangled, overflowed, and unwalkable piece of forest"—the Okefenokee Swamp. He reached Florida, his "flowery Canaan," finding the land "so watery and vine-tied that pathless wanderings are not easily possible." Attempts to plow straight ahead left Muir "tangled in a labyrinth of armed vines like a fly in a spider-web."

And yet he stuck to the wilderness, drinking "from slimy pools groped for in the grass" and somehow keeping his bearings through serpentine waterways: "No stream that I crossed to-day appeared to have the least idea where it was going." After only eight days, he reached Florida's west coast and the Gulf of Mexico, its briny scent kindling memories of old Dunbar. In the town of Cedar Key, he learned he would have to wait two weeks for the schooner to Galveston, and found interim work at a lumber mill.

Soon after taking the job, Muir "felt a strange dullness and headache. . . . Thinking that a bath in the salt water might refresh me, I plunged in and swam a little distance, but this seemed only to make me feel worse." Two days later, "the fever broke on me like a storm, and before I had staggered halfway to the mill I fell down unconscious on the narrow trail."

That malarial fever brought Muir near death; only after three months of nursing did he feel well enough to walk. During

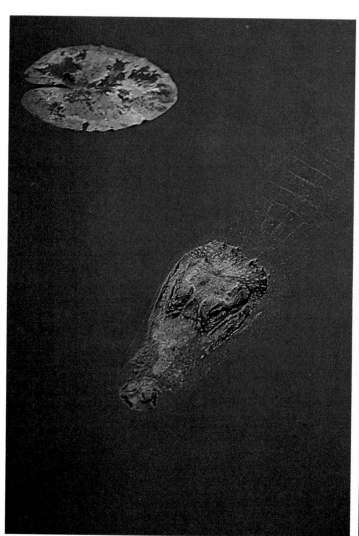

Without a ripple to warn its prey, an alligator glides silently through a Florida swamp. Muir kept a wary watch for these powerful reptiles as he splashed and hiked from Fernandina Beach through murky waters and forests to the Gulf of Mexico. Nothing in Muir's travels had prepared him for the "magnificent realm" of Florida's interior, teeming with strange plants and wild creatures. Gleaming like patent leather, a yellow rat snake raises its head above a curled body. Fiddler crabs scurry on the rich crumbly soil of a marshland floor. With long tongues, butterflies gather nectar from wild flowers.

CLOUDLESS SULPHUR

GULF FRITILLARY

this prolonged convalescence, he pondered again his place in the universe.

He balked at the common belief, then, that earth's bounty existed solely for man's enjoyment. Sheep, because they provided man with clothing and food, ate grass "by divine appointment for this predestined purpose.... In the same pleasant plan, whales are storehouses of oil for us ... hemp ... is a case of evident destination for ships' rigging, wrapping packages, and hanging the wicked.... Iron was made for hammers and ploughs, and lead for bullets."

If so, reasoned Muir, then perhaps man was intended for alligators or insects, because he serves them as completely as sheep do us.

But no! "These are unresolvable difficulties connected with Eden's apple and the Devil. Why does water drown its lord? Why do so many minerals poison him? Why are so many plants and fishes deadly enemies? Why is the lord of creation subjected to the same laws of life as his subjects?"

The Creator, believed Muir, made the earth not for man alone, but for all His family. True, "The universe would be incomplete without man; but it would also be incomplete without the smallest transmicroscopic creature that dwells beyond our conceitful eyes and knowledge."

And so Muir's cosmic eye foresaw the import of ecology — the science of togetherness — that all living things are related, and to toy with one affects all others. What had begun as a straightforward shakedown for tropical adventure now ended as a forge for Muir's belief in the unity of the cosmos. Still, he could not forget Humboldt. He sailed to Cuba, waited a month for his remnant fever to subside and a southbound boat to depart. Neither occurred.

Convinced that "All the world was before me and every day was a holiday," he settled on a new destination — California — as the best climate for his health and love of botany. His thoughts turned to the American West — and a place with the entrancing name of Yosemite Valley.

Dying rays of the sun burnish the shallows as glossy ibises feed near Cedar Key, Florida. Muir reached this island town — and the end of his thousand-mile walk — on October 23, 1867, intending to embark immediately for Cuba. A severe attack of malaria forced him to delay his departure.

3

YOSEMITE AND THE RANGE OF LIGHT

Cloud-swept sunset lights the steeply plunging gorge of California's Yosemite Valley in the Sierra Nevada; Half Dome towers at right. Muir's sketch illustrates his theory that glaciers shaped Half Dome. Muir first came to the Valley in 1868, and found it "the grandest of all the special temples of Nature I was ever permitted to enter...." He continually returned to this enchanting wilderness.

MUIR RODE STEERAGE to Panama, crossed the isthmus, and sailed to San Francisco, a city he enjoyed no more than he had Louisville. Its disquieting rush and bustle prompted an immediate quest for the quickest way out of town. "But where do you want to go?" he was asked. "To any place that is wild," Muir replied. He was directed to Oakland.

He reached Oakland—and kept heading east, joyously botanizing during April 1868 through California's Central Valley, "the floweriest piece of world I ever walked." Blossoms stretched solidly before him "like a lake of pure sunshine" 50 miles wide. While he exulted in these vast "bee pastures," Muir's eyes were drawn constantly to a miragelike ribbon of mountains. The rugged, burnished range hovered before his gaze "miles in height . . . and so gloriously colored, and so luminous, it seems to be not clothed with light, but wholly composed of it, like the wall of some celestial city." In 1776, Pedro Font, a Spanish priest, had named the snow-belted chain the Sierra Nevada, or "Snowy Range." But the pure, radiant beauty of these granite peaks elicited from Muir another description— "The Range of Light."

As he clambered into the Sierra foothills, "mountain winds and delicious crystal water" cooled his chronic fevers. Muir rediscovered his mountaineer's soul: "We are now in the mountains and they are in us, kindling enthusiasm, making every nerve quiver, filling every pore and cell." Following forest-lined mountain trails, Muir climbed higher into the Sierra Nevada; suddenly, a deep valley enclosed by colossal steeps and mighty waterfalls yawned before him. Spellbound, he entered Yosemite Valley.

At once, its "grandeur and the spiritual glow" so engulfed him that he "shouted and gesticulated in a wild burst of ecstasy." His words later flowed as fast as Yosemite cascades: "The whole landscape showed design, like man's noblest sculptures." Canyons became "mountain streets full of life and light"; the river spoke "with a thousand songful voices"; Yosemite seemed "an immense hall or temple lighted from above," where "Nature had gathered her choicest treasures."

For ten days, Muir wandered, marveling, through this spectacular defile. But the need for a job soon drove him back down the mountain. He ended up in the town of Snelling, where he found work first as a harvest hand, then as a sheepshearer and shepherd's helper.

His job with the shepherd—washing a few pans and baking bread—left him free time throughout the spring and summer of 1869 to roam the mountains, discover new plants and animals, sketch peaks, and scale canyon walls. Finally, in the fall of that year, he returned to Yosemite, and again he was entranced. He found the Valley "a tree-lover's paradise" framed by "noble walls—sculptured into endless variety of domes and gables, spires and battlements and plain mural precipices—all a-tremble with the thunder tones of the falling water." Muir can be forgiven these literary excesses, for truly Yosemite is astounding, a vast and varied land. Its unforgettable skyline of Half Dome, Glacier Point, and El Capitan sends the heart soaring.

And sometimes, it propels far more than the heart. At dawn one clear day, I watched in disbelief as four young adults took turns running off the precipice of Glacier Point—hitched onto nylon hang gliders hardly more substantial than the air. It all seemed a little unreal, this mountaintop bustling with sky sailors so early in the morning. The lone woman kept urging her dawdling male companions to hurry while the updrafts were strong, because "we won't be able to make a second flight."

Finally, hard hat in place and glider on her back, she trotted down the gradual "runway," perhaps a dozen steps to the sheer face of Glacier Point. Just before the edge, where I expected her to stop from fear—or to plummet over the precipice—the nylon sail filled as if by magic. Suddenly, her still-running feet churned empty air. She was airborne.

More than a half-mile below her lay the green expanse of the Valley. A mile away loomed the magnificent granite bulk of Half Dome, Muir's "most beautiful and most sublime of all the wonderful Yosemite rocks." Waterfalls—Yosemite, Vernal, Nevada—crashed down the cliffs. The bright yellow and blue hang glider coursed among these marvels, slowly spiraling to the earth.

Had John Muir lived in the age of hang gliders, I have no doubt he would have followed that young woman off Glacier Point to drift effortlessly among the morning breezes. He loved a good adventure almost as much as he loved nature; to him the two were often inseparable.

During one climb alongside Yosemite Falls, Muir's eye for thrills spotted a narrow rock shelf at the very brink of the torrent. Stuffing his mouth with bitter herbs "to keep caution keen and prevent giddiness," he sidestepped out onto that shelf, hands groping across the flat rock face. One slip and he would have joined the waterfall—tumbling down to its granite base far below. His reward for taking such a chance? A staggering view of the roiling, charging spume as it chuted past his heels in a "bright irised throng of comet-like streamers."

Another spectacular ledge, Sunnyside Bench, was one of Muir's favorite observatories of Yosemite Falls. Although broader than the other shelf, Sunnyside Bench still delighted Muir with its risky closeness to nature's power; he believed that "One must labor for beauty as for bread." With some trepidation I set out to find Sunnyside Bench.

My climb began on steep talus—a loose jumble of sharp, broken boulders accumulated at the base of a cliff. One stone caught my total attention. Looking as fresh as yesterday was a

Yosemite National Park sprawls across the west slope of the Sierra Nevada. The Park holds towering mountains, sparkling lakes, rivers with foaming waterfalls, huge granite formations, and groves of giant sequoias. An Act of Congress in 1890 established the Park; with the later creation of Sequoia and Kings Canyon National Parks (below), much of the Sierra—Muir's Range of Light—became federally protected land.

bit of felt-pen graffiti: "J. Muir 7/4/83." Why the wag who had written this picked that date, I don't know. But if Muir had tramped this way in 1883, he would have inhaled, as I did, the pungent fragrance of California laurel—the bay leaf so essential to stews and soups. Manzanita blooms also perfumed the air—while the plant's tough, barkless limbs clawed at mine. I climbed higher, and soon Yosemite Falls—a series of three roaring cataracts of rainbowed mountain mist—crashed before me. During the 2,425 feet of its plummet, winds and gravity atomize the water into droplets, marshaling them into pulsing stalactites that merge, diverge, and almost seem to melt into the air.

I let my mind wander, trying to visualize myself as a single speck of water riding that streaming, foaming roller coaster. I drifted slowly at first with a million comrades, then gathered speed, and finally crashed into the rocks at the bottom of the falls. After that wild flight with its tumultuous finale, I imagined floating happily down the gentle Merced River all the way to the Pacific Ocean.

Muir would have reveled in just such a ride; it suited his uncommonly cosmic vision, which could find endless wonderment in a snowflake or grasshopper wing. Throughout his life, he remained something of a little boy, full of a child's admiration for the universe, a child's energy, and a child's ability to outlast cold, accident, and danger.

Muir's almost superhuman tenacity to endure and even enjoy hardship soon became legend. I had hoped a similar inner toughness would lead me in triumph to Sunnyside Bench. But a snow-laden cloud sailed down the Valley, blotting out trees and even part of the falls. I surrendered to common sense, and turned back.

On another day, I set out for one of Yosemite's gentler splendors, Mirror Lake, a quiet, blossomlike swelling on the stalk of Tenaya Creek. With me was Dana Morgenson, hiker and photographer, who has spent 31 years in Yosemite.

"I've been here longer than John Muir," he said with a grin. "I like to think I know Yosemite pretty well. But the trails are never quite the same—the light will be different, a tree will fall, or the moss green up. It's always changing." He compared Yosemite's majesties to an unlimited number of doors. "Open one and you're faced with countless others."

Our first door that day opened on a winding trail that led us along the clear waters of Tenaya Creek, stained in places by iron oxide. What magic there is in wilderness, I thought, that even rust can be beautiful, a startling counterpoint to the lush green riverbank. Even the rocks seemed fertile, strung with soggy green tendrils of moss. We threaded among tall Douglas firs, incense cedars, and large ponderosa pines—nicknamed "puzzle pines" for their bark, which flakes off piecemeal in jigsaw-puzzle shapes. Here and there, a giant of the forest lay uprooted, blown over by the occasional "Mono wind" that roars down Tenaya Canyon.

We struggled up a slope of house-size boulders. Somewhere below, I heard the music of snowmelt traveling some hidden channel among the rocks. Muir loved climbing on talus; he would skip across the bare, uneven rockpiles as easily as if they were cobbles, his feet tapping out a rhythm to match the water's melody below.

Much of the talus we walked had fallen from Half Dome above us. As distinctive as Gibraltar, this once-spherical mountain of granite was sheared in two millenniums ago, leaving one immense flat face falling sheer to the Valley floor. It captivates the eye from any angle, as does a diamond rotating slowly in a jeweler's window.

Near its base lies Mirror Lake, which we reached just as an oncoming drizzle dappled its emerald surface with spreading circles. The shower was so light that the sun stayed out, transforming the misty drops into a gilded veil. Spongelike mosses drank in the wetness; spring's first spikes of grass poked through the mat of last year's pine needles. Everywhere lay the smell of life, dampness, the earth.

My hand dipped into the lake for a submerged oak leaf, so decayed that only its network of veins remained. Tiny lenses of water clung to this filigree that once had served living cells, wherein miniature green factories transformed carbon dioxide and water into sugar. I marveled at this alchemy of photosynthesis. Nature outfits each leaf with millions of these food-making factories, and thousands of leaves crown a single oak. And each towering oak originates from a single cell, a microscopic bit of protoplasm within the developing acorn.

Muir's first summer in the Sierra—when he worked for a shepherd—generated similar quiet revelations. Human concepts of space and time faded to nothingness: "No pain here, no dull empty hours, no fear of the past, no fear of the future. These blessed mountains are so compactly filled with God's beauty, no petty personal hope or experience has room to be."

Muir gave up sheepherding, despising his flock as "hoofed locusts" for mindlessly cropping his beloved mountain flowers. Instead, he took to rambling by himself.

The Range of Light entranced him with the desolate beauty of its mysteriously rounded, almost lumpy peaks. Canyons glistened with a strange, "smooth-wiped appearance." He began to wonder why this was so. Suddenly, an answer leaped to his mind—glaciers! Ancient, massive rivers of ice had slowly overswept the Sierra and sculpted deep valleys such as Yosemite. "A FINE DISCOVERY THIS!" he exulted.

Although not the first to hypothesize on Yosemite's glacial origins, he popularized the theory so energetically that others soon called it "Muir's discovery." Glaciers became his "glorious work." He preached his glacial sermon to Yosemite visitors, pointing out ice-caused scars and polish on the granite as he spouted, "Religion is on all the rocks."

Eastern scientists—including Dr. Clinton Merriam of the Smithsonian Institution in Washington, D. C., and John Runkle, president of the Massachusetts Institute of Technology—traveled west to seek out this shaggy sage and beg him to write up his findings. Muir's thoughts disputed the published views of California State Geologist Josiah D. Whitney, who credited Yosemite to some sudden, catastrophic collapse. Whitney's name and reputation were prestigious—and his credentials included a Harvard professorship. He dismissed Muir's theory as the ravings of a mere sheepherder. True, Muir had worked as a sheepherder and was a college dropout. He also underestimated the effects of uplift and water erosion. But basically, he was right, and his theory scientifically sound.

Muir's determination to be heard helped forge his burgeoning reputation as an eloquent visionary. Harvard botanist Asa Gray trekked the Sierra with him, encouraged his botanical explorations, and even used his name for a plant — *Ivesia muirii*, commonly called mousetails.

Another, entirely different pilgrim to Muir's shrine was novelist Therése Yelverton, who later wrote *Zanita*, a sentimental and barely-fictionalized tale about Yosemite. Its mountain-man hero is named Kenmuir, "a peculiar looking object" who laughingly runs up the barest ledges and walls "with the cautious activity of a goat, never losing for a moment the rhythmic motion of his flexile form." His "bright intelligent face" beams with "open blue eyes . . . and glorious auburn hair" — as did Muir's. His "garments had the tatterdemalion style of a Mad Tom. The waist of his trousers was eked out with a grass band; a long flowing sedge rush stuck in the solitary buttonhole of his shirt, the sleeves of which were ragged and forlorn, and his shoes appeared to have known hard and troublous times." Kenmuir, like John Muir, would eagerly climb gigantic pines "to reach some particular cone, and point out its wonderful structure."

Although she did not cast herself as heroine, Mrs. Yelverton could not escape an attraction to the model for her hero, about whom she wrote after leaving Yosemite: "My dear Kenmuir, How I have wished for you . . . I never see a beautiful flower . . . in nature without thinking of you." Such romantic advances apparently drew no favorable response from the nature-infatuated Muir. It would take a person of totally different ilk to impress him.

O NE MORNING, Muir was toiling at a sawmill in Yosemite Valley — the job he took after leaving the shepherd. A serene and rather frail old man rode up on horseback and asked to see him. The young, rustic sawyer was stunned; he would recall the experience many years later as one of the greatest moments of his life. There stood his saint, the aging sage Ralph Waldo Emerson, whose essays on nature Muir had greedily devoured since his university days. Emerson, the author of such lines as "In the woods is perpetual youth," and ". . . if a man would be alone, let him look at the stars," had come to meet Muir, encouraged by a mutual friend. Muir's initial shyness broke away in a flood of exhilaration at having both his ideals — Emerson and Yosemite — together. He brought forth his most valued possessions — dried plant specimens and sketches — by the score, begging Emerson to accept them. Two days later, they left with a mounted party for the Mariposa Grove of sequoias south of Yosemite Valley. *(Continued on page 88)*

81

"...into this one mountain mansion Nature had gathered her choicest treasures..."

Hushed majesty over-spreads the wild flowers, waterfalls, and granite cliffs of Yosemite Valley, which, to Muir, seemed "an immense hall or temple lighted from above." For some five years, Muir centered his life here, exploring the meadows and mountains, and observing flora such as the showy milkweed (top left). He filled long journals with his reflections and sketches— and with an occasional pressed plant.

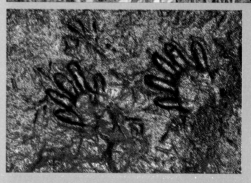

Cottony clouds rim the heights above Yosemite Valley, glistening in the summer sun. The play of light in the mountains entranced Muir; he wrote of the Sierra, "it seems to be not clothed with light, but wholly composed of it, like the wall of some celestial city." Massive walls and steep defiles mark Yosemite; Muir's century-old sketch (far left) matches a vista of today (top left). For decades, Muir worked to preserve his beloved Yosemite, haven for such wild things as a raccoon which left its tracks in river mud.

"The winter clouds grow, and bloom, and shed their starry crystals on every leaf and rock..."

Snow-decked clumps of grass pattern a boggy meadow beneath Half Dome, "the most beautiful and most sublime of all the wonderful Yosemite rocks." The ferocity of Yosemite's winters captivated Muir as totally as the tranquillity of its summers. Mist drifts across the face of El Capitan—a solitary rampart of granite—evoking Muir's thought that "the clouds come and go among the cliffs like living creatures."

Muir delighted in identifying the sugar pines, firs, and incense cedars for his new companion as they slowly rode toward the famed "Big Trees." Wrote a friend of Emerson's: "at first they seemed not so very big. We grew curious, and . . . soon began to discover what company we were in." One fallen trunk spanned 19 feet in diameter, another more than 30. At a living monarch called the Grizzly Giant, "we found that our thirteen horses were not enough; it would need about six more to compass it."

Emerson was duly impressed by Muir and his sequoias. "The wonder is that we can see these trees and not wonder more!" Decades later, Muir would recall, "Emerson was the most serene, majestic, sequoia-like soul I ever met." The two naturalists planned to camp that night among the big trees, but the others discouraged the 68-year-old Emerson from an experience they feared would strain his constitution. Muir alone begged him to stay: "It is as if a photographer should remove his plate before the impression was fully made." Emerson sadly declined; after lunch, he and the party left Muir alone with his congregation of giant trees.

I SENSED A LONELINESS similar to Muir's when I entered Mariposa Grove, for it was wrapped in the silence of early spring, remote from the crowds that would fill it in summer. A winter's worth of snow blocked the road with some five feet of white; but it was packed hard enough to hike atop for the two miles to the grove. With me was Bill Kimes, a Muir bibliographer, who lives in the nearby town of Mariposa. We talked as we trudged through the steepening snows, but not freely. My heart felt the exertion; veins stood out on the backs of my hands. I grew conscious of an effort to slow my voice and not reveal how deeply I was having to breathe. After all, I reflected, this was my first lengthy high-country hike since leaving the rolling hills of the Appalachians.

Passing sugar pines and incense cedars, we approached our first sequoias. "Some young ones there," Bill remarked, pointing to symmetrical, flaky-barked trunks several feet thick. "Probably only a couple centuries old. Muir used to say the sequoia was the only tree that stayed around long enough to get hit by lightning—all the old ones have been topped."

True to Bill's words, many sequoias we saw lacked the tapering head of youth. Even so, they were divinely beautiful. We might have been walking down the gallery of a Gothic cathedral. Majestic pillars stood bold on either side, dappled and burnished by shafts of sunlight that penetrated the leafy canopy overhead. This light seemed warm and glowing, as if it had been filtered through stained glass. Over all, I sensed a noble hush. My ears groped for sound, any sound, seizing upon the slightest birdcall or faintest murmur of the wind and treasuring it long after it had faded to silence. How quiet, how serene, how sacred this grove seemed to me.

Like Emerson's companions, I did not feel the greatness of these trees at once, not until I went up to the Grizzly Giant and tried to encircle its scarred old trunk with my arms. It's like hugging a barn. The immensity of these trees overtook me only when I was less than an arm's length away.

I found it amusing that sequoias should sprout walnut-size cones — small for any conifer, but especially for this goliath, the largest living plant in the world. I marveled at the centuries that this patient mountaineer before me had held its vigil. I wondered how many storms it had weathered, what tales it could tell. I hesitated, wistfully hoping that it could speak to me. But there was no sound, not even that of windblown branches rubbing together.

Mariposa Grove, like Yosemite Valley, today is included in the 761,000-acre Yosemite National Park. Muir energetically worked for the creation of such a preserve, for he saw the area endangered by timbering and grazing interests, which only the federal government could deter. Today, many visitors to the Park are alarmed when they see small fires flickering in the nationally-protected forests — and astonished when they find out that these blazes were set by Park employees! But, I quickly learned, fire helps preserve Yosemite's forests and meadows, just as it helped create them centuries ago.

"We wouldn't try to stop a volcano from erupting — a natural fire's the same sort of thing," said Dr. Jan van Wagtendonk, Park research scientist. He explained that fires regularly swept Yosemite long before the first pioneers came, clearing it of duff — pine needles, bark, cones, and other forest tinder — and the countless new seedlings that would otherwise fill the meadowed valley with trees. But throughout the early days of the Park, a policy of strict preservationism kept all fires — even natural ones — out of the Valley. Duff built up over the decades to explosive proportions. At the same time, original tree populations changed.

"John Muir saw colonnades of big trees in Yosemite, with lots of open ground in between them. Since then we've had an invasion of pines and cedars that fires normally would have controlled. If you wanted to re-create Muir's Yosemite instantly, you'd have to log over those excess trees — but I don't think our public is ready for that," Jan said smiling. Instead, Park work crews have recently begun burning some 1,000 acres each year in small, controlled blazes that clear out unwanted debris and seedlings without harming mature, established trees. "We'd like to increase it to about 10,000 acres yearly — we've a lot of catching up to do."

One controlled fire I saw put to rest any fears spawned by a Smokey-the-Bear upbringing; an ordinary autumn leaf-burning would have outclassed it. We easily walked faster than the flames could burn—as did the wildlife. Such fires, in fact, benefit some animals. Jan sees "a lot of coyotes in fields after a burn —they're looking for meadow mice."

Fire also clears out underbrush, stimulating new growth of berry bushes—the natural food for Yosemite's bears. This helps to relieve their dependency on man. For generations, the Park's black bears grew bold begging food from tourists. Now, they steal from campers and backpackers and ransack garbage sites. They cause as much as a hundred thousand dollars in property damage each year.

"Bears are very trendy animals," biologist Dave Graber explained one day in Yosemite. "They copy each other. Last year a lot of them broke in car windows to get at food inside. But the bears in Sequoia National Park—200 miles south of here—didn't do that at all. I'm willing to bet the Yosemite bears got into the habit just by watching each other."

Like every national park, Yosemite attempts to maintain a natural ecosystem, and so rangers move bears away from developed regions to more remote areas within the Park. Problem bruins that continue to return may be destroyed.

To find better ways of handling Yosemite's bears, Dave and his small research team are intensively studying the shaggy mammals. "Black bear ecology is fairly well known—but not the specifics of the bears here," he explained. "We don't know how many there are, what they eat, whether they move seasonally. We don't even know if the bears we catch are residents or transients from outside the Park."

Dave's program of tagging the bears should help eliminate such confusion. So far, he has tagged more than 140 bears, perhaps one-third of the Park's total. In addition to tags, Dave assigns them names—"They're easier to remember than numbers." Dave's list includes: Kong—weighed in at 350 pounds; Rocky Raccoon—dark, raccoonlike eye circles; and Adios— the one that got away.

One morning, I accompanied Dave to one of his portable, barrel-shaped bear traps and peeked through a small opening at its sedated occupant. I watched as Dave and assistant Bob Hare opened the steel drum and poured out a large ball of dark brown fur.

"He's big!" Dave exclaimed. "One of the half-dozen largest black bears I've seen. Well over 300 pounds. By November, he'll weigh a hundred pounds more."

The three of us then rolled this monster onto a stretcher so Dave could take blood samples for analysis and Bob could tag his ear for identification. Small, frightened-looking eyes stared up at us; a furry jaw shook uncontrollably.

Visiting Yosemite in 1871 at the age
of 68, philosopher-writer Ralph
Waldo Emerson listens to his young
disciple, John Muir, as the two
stand solemnly among towering
sequoias in the Mariposa Grove.
After a moment of quiet reverence,
the frail man, whose writings had
long inspired Muir, spoke with
awe: "There were giants in those
days." Muir replied, "You are
yourself a sequoia. Stop and get
acquainted with your big brethren."
But Emerson departed, hurried
away by friends concerned for his
health. To a short list of men he had
known who had most influenced
him, he added the name "John Muir."

"But because of the sedation," Dave explained, "he's insensitive to pain, and too disorganized to be really frightened." The bear's misshapen jaw—an old break that had healed poorly—dictated the name Snaggletooth. It also accentuated his helplessness. Flat on his back and shaking, this monarch of the forest could neither move nor fight. Even his capture had been a study in defeat.

"He was climbing around some tents," Dave said, "when a ranger spotted him and opened the door to the trap—he walked right in without a struggle!" Such peaceable and unexpected behavior pleases Dave, a 27-year-old candidate for a doctorate in wildlife biology, who so loves bears that he "wanted to get one to officiate" at his wedding later that week. His interest in bears is relatively recent, however, following stints in politics and journalism. "I feel that what I'm doing here matters—that's a good feeling. Going into wildlife at first was like going back to childhood—as a kid, I related to animals better than to people. I guess I still do."

Such words might have come from Muir, who said, ". . . if a war of races should occur between the wild beasts and Lord Man, I would be tempted to sympathize with the bears."

Today, people are the main problem in Yosemite National Park, simply because of their sheer numbers. Crowds—even the best behaved ones—threaten the very solitude and beauty that beckon them. Even with a shuttle-bus service that keeps many cars off the roads, there is still a summer glut of traffic and people; 99 percent of the two million annual visitors crunch into 1 percent of the Park—Yosemite Valley. They line up for gas, food, supplies, even for views at each scenic overlook. Add to these hordes the steamy temperatures of summer and it is easy to understand why Dave Graber terms summer "the most unpleasant time in the Valley."

But even in summer, even in the Valley, I found that I could escape the crowds by fleeing to the Merced, well-named River of Mercy. Although this stream threads through the heart of the populous Valley, it remains almost deserted. Apparently, most tourists out to sightsee overlook the sight closest to them—the river.

I decided to tour the Merced by inner tube—a big truck-size one. I found pure joy in floating on the green waters of the Merced and letting the soothing scenery roll by. The river served as nature's own tour bus, taking me past the Valley's splendors at a relaxed pace and letting me get on and off where I pleased—it was even air-conditioned and free of mosquitoes!

For the first few hundred yards, I was entirely alone with blue skies, green trees, and those fantastic granite cliffs that seem even grander when mirrored in the water. Rocks along the river picked up so much reflected light that they glowed with hues of copper and gold. I coasted around a bend and watched a lone old fisherman fly-casting the pools and eddies for trout. The bright-speckled fish darted everywhere through the deep, clear water. They were small, only six or eight inches long, but they were numerous.

As I swirled downstream, the river passed under footbridges and picked up more people, but nothing like the hurried crush on the Valley's roads. I encountered only sunbathers, swimmers, more inner-tubers like me, and yet no one seemed to be in the way — of each other or of the Merced's natural beauty. I could smell the woods' piny fragrance, hear the rustle of black cottonwood leaves. Clearings along the riverside gave spectacular views of Valley landmarks. I still remember Cathedral Rocks awash in alpenglow, the three-pronged crag a burning magnet for sunlight, while darkness and half-shadows engulfed the rest of the Valley. Along some stretches, heavy woods walled the river tightly, blocking out noise and summer mobs. The isolation was near perfect. My single complaint was that the sun set way too soon.

"Handsomest building in the Valley," Muir proudly wrote of his first Yosemite home, a one-room cabin of pine logs that he and a friend built near Yosemite Falls in 1869.

Muir's penchant for simplicity once inspired him to float the Merced — downriver from Yosemite — on a raft of warped fence boards. Had inner tubes been available, I'm sure he would have tried this simplest of conveyances.

Apart from floating the Merced, there is another way to escape summer congestion in the Valley — climb out of it. Just one highway channels park traffic east to west; on either side stretch miles of absolutely roadless wilderness, much of it High Sierra — the realm of bare, rocky peaks lofting high above timberline. Here, Muir spent many summer days scrambling about the granite monuments that glaciers had carved into domes, mesas, waves, and whaleback curves. Just below the mountainous source of the Merced and Tuolumne Rivers, he relished what he considered "the brightest of all Sierra landscapes," and excitedly found a living glacier — the first discovered in the Sierra. At last, he had found the long-sought proof of his glacial theory, which not even Josiah Whitney could dispute. Additional evidence followed, from other dying glaciers and from Tenaya Lake, liquid remnant of a long-disappeared river of ice northeast of Yosemite Valley. Miwok Indians called the lake Py-we-ak, or "lake of shining rocks." Muir correctly explained the shine as glacial polish, the result of almost unimaginable pressure from icy rivers bearing down through the centuries, crushing and *(Continued on page 99)*

Harnessed to his nylon hang glider, a sky sailor floats downward on gentle morning winds toward Yosemite Valley. He launched himself by simply running off the precipice of Glacier Point. The spiraling descent of more than 3,000 feet lasts about 20 minutes; Park officials regulate the sport.

On a cold spring day, California gulls swoop
down to pluck food from the ice-glazed waters
of Tenaya Lake. Tenaya and hundreds of other
lakes scattered throughout the Sierra Nevada
mark the pathways of ancient glaciers that
once covered the highlands. The heavy glaciers
ground across the landscape, smoothing and
polishing rock surfaces, from small boulders to
entire mountains, like Polly Dome (above) on
Tenaya's shore. Because of the luster of the
rocks around this lake, Miwok Indians called
it Py-we-ak, "lake of shining rocks." Muir, who
spent years tracing and studying the work of
glaciers, noted with wonder that "out of all the
cold darkness and glacial crushing and grinding comes this warm, abounding beauty...."

Mono Lake, east of
Yosemite, reflects an
azure shore and a violet
sky on a waning winter
afternoon. Islands of
reef-like tufa, deposits
of calcium carbonate, jut
from the mineral-charged
lake. Muir sketched
nearby mountains (right),
and described the area
as a "country of
wonderful contrasts."

E. flank of the Sierra, from bank of Rush Creek.
near Mono.

eroding and buffing the rocks to their present smooth finish.

Today, the region is the picture of serenity. Well-muscled peaks that survived glacial onslaughts rise ruggedly above the blueness of Tenaya Lake. Brilliantly clear waters reveal every grain of sand on the bottom. I found it refreshing simply to sit and gaze at the depths, and watch the rocks there bounce light around as might a prism.

Just east of the lake lies the Park's main high-country attraction—Tuolumne Meadows, largest glacial meadow in all the Sierra. The Pacific Crest Trail, a high-elevation backpacking path that runs the length of California, Oregon, and Washington, is called the John Muir Trail in this section of the Sierra. It crosses the flowery Meadows and leads south nearly 200 miles to Mount Whitney, named in honor of geologist Josiah Whitney. Near that peak, the John Muir Wilderness, Muir Pass, and Mount Muir memorialize the man who spent a decade exploring the area. Indeed, more California place-names commemorate Muir than anyone else, even George Washington.

The central location of Tuolumne Meadows campground makes it a high-country headquarters for thousands of backpackers, rock climbers, and horsemen each year. But once out of camp it is still possible to travel Yosemite's backcountry for days—even weeks—and encounter few other people. Muir would like that. He usually traveled solo, believing that "Only by going alone in silence, without baggage, can one truly get into the heart of the wilderness. All other travel is mere dust and hotels and baggage and chatter."

Eager to test his philosophy, I set out from the Meadows along the Tuolumne River—the even less-traveled sister of the Merced—rambling there alone, afoot, and unencumbered by gear. For food, I carried only some tea, sugar, and bread. Muir relied on such mountain rations again and again—partly because they helped keep expenses down to a few dollars. But even when he had money, his diet remained the same. Mind-soaring scenery provided his only dessert.

Underfoot spread Tuolumne Meadows' broad, flowery lawn, thousands of blossoms so small and dense that I could not help treading on dozens with each step. Light breezes brushed the grassy nap at my feet, rippling through gentle heather, tiny shooting stars, and the luscious, liquid yellow of buttercups that bowed and danced like marionettes. These are happy meadows, laced by bright clear streams and cheered by playful chipmunks and birds by the score: robins, finches, nuthatches, and jays.

A deep blue sky set off the pinnacles of Cathedral and Unicorn Peaks—still snow-tipped in mid-July. Before me spread the transparent and shining Tuolumne River. Deer tracks abounded; perfumed groves of lodgepole pines alternated with the hot, sunny Meadows. The Range of Light is indeed the sun's realm, I thought. Even the placid river I followed seemed more sky than water, for it reflected the cloudless heavens perfectly—one continuous expanse of blue.

But soon, this quiet Tuolumne left the embrace of flat meadow and pine grove to sing out its name in foamy waterfalls. It tumbled down stair-stepping cascades, each following the last with increased steepness, the river seeming to rejoice in new life and freedom. Above the spume I found a perfect view of 12,590-foot Mount Conness, some seven miles distant. As with most Sierra peaks, trees covered its granite skeleton only sparsely, like tufting on furniture. No thick green skin obscured the mountain's tough, bare bones.

Near Glen Aulin—"beautiful valley" in Gaelic—churning, splashing falls so mesmerized me that I did not hear an upcoming pack train until the muleskinner politely asked me to move from the middle of the trail. He was bringing the day's supplies to a nearby camp.

I could have hired a mule or horse for this trek, I thought. But walking yields a greater closeness to the earth, an independence. The solid thud of boots on the path means freedom to stop and admire a flower, to move at one's own speed, to rejoice in crossing a stream on risky stepping-stones, to explore off the trail, to get a close-up view of dew jeweling the grass. Besides, the Tuolumne is all downhill!

At Waterwheel Falls, the path threaded among granite rocks and an increasingly rugged landscape. Sheets of foam splashed about as the river rose up in great rooster tails. At the Third Cascade of Waterwheel Falls, a shelf of granite—upturned like the tip of a ski—shot fountains of spray skyward in a spectacular natural display.

Just as the river began to quiet below Waterwheel, canyon walls reared up tall and powerful in the bold magnificence of sheer rock. This was the start of the Grand Canyon of the Tuolumne—which includes a section known as Muir Gorge.

I was so cheered by the good day and the progress I had made that I decided to leave the regular trail and poke about in the brush. Not five feet off the path, I encountered the hardest bushwhacking of my life. Tenacious, low-growing manzanita grabbed out at my unprotected legs with taloned branches. Dead or alive, it is the hiker's archenemy. Lifeless branches, bleached though they may be, retain all the snags and spring of their live brethren. Try to smash one underfoot and another always snaps up, jabbing the legs or slashing the skin. I thrashed in one direction, then another—and another—but every lead proved false: nothing but dead ends full of manzanita. Defeated, I returned to the trail.

Double and triple layers of granite palisades stood out proudly above me, buttressed more solidly than any man-made fortress. I paused for a drink, dipping my tin cup into the fast-paced Tuolumne. I gulped cup after cup of sparkling water from this river that seemed so clear and pure.

There is an indefinable freedom and joy in this simple act of drinking from a mountain stream. No chlorine, fluoride, or sewage taints its cool, utterly tasteless water. To drink here is to reaffirm the bond between man and nature. I felt thankful that such elemental pleasures were still mine to enjoy. I almost expected a tousled John Muir to appear, guide the way through manzanita tangles, and point out the alpenglow as the sun westered home.

Following the trail up several granite knobs a few hundred feet above the water, I gloried in the sunset from the top of the second knob—and then realized that I had better make camp fast. Darkness comes quickly to the Range of Light.

Suddenly, I was lost. The trail melted into underbrush. I retraced my steps and tried to go forward once more, without success. I thought about following the sound of the river—but I feared that I would fall in. I knew it would be impossible to blaze my own way to White Wolf, perhaps fifteen miles away, through that manzanita. But I could not stay put either; there wasn't even room to sleep. I headed west—the direction the trail was taking me before I lost it—bushwhacked through a thicket, crossed two streamlets, and there was the path, reappearing as suddenly as it had evaporated. Thankful, I followed the path down to the river and picked out a flat rock on which I could heat water for tea.

Dinnertime! After twelve hours of walking and no food, I should have been ravenous. But strangely I wasn't. Nor did I have hallucinations of thick, sputtering steaks. I ate my bread and sipped my tea slowly—and truly enjoyed the meal, amazed at how little is required to be content here. Of course birdcalls and mountain beauty could never erase my daily need for food. But how else could I explain an empty but satisfied stomach? It did not just tolerate a full day of fasting; it felt *good*. My senses seemed elevated, too, perhaps as much by the lack of food as by the uplifting scenery. Maybe that's why Muir stuck to his bread-and-tea diet.

For me, one of the greatest pleasures of the wilderness comes in the morning—with the predawn stillness, the winging of birds overhead. I lay there, warm and rested, looking out on a land totally reversed from the night before. Mountains that were mere silhouettes in sunset's fading light now jutted solidly; the foreground cliff that was so ruggedly three-dimensional now seemed as empty of depth as a stage flat. Morning's first rays revealed a Sierra forest sparse and thin, not the fearsome thick blackness I recalled. Alpenglow roused the mountaintops, the Tuolumne chuckled as birds chirped in tune—who could be anything but happy on such a day?

But the sun seemed to lag; slowly its light dawdled down

"Climb the mountains and get their good tidings," urged Muir, a lifelong mountaineer who often scaled dangerously steep heights on his many rambles through the Sierra. Precipitous rock walls—typical formations throughout the Range of Light—mark the southern Sierra near Mount Whitney. The high,

escarpment of the range resulted from a series of upheavals beneath the earth's surface millions of years ago. These disturbances lifted a great block of the earth's crust sharply upward, then tilted it on its side as other blocks sank down. This huge tilted block became the long rocky spine of the Sierra.

the canyon walls. As I lay in my sleeping bag, waiting, the feeling slowly overtook me that everything else—the birds, the plants, even the rocks—also seemed to be waiting for the sun's appearance. Then, suddenly, sunlight broke upon me, and I rejoiced in its warmth and brightness. Trees filtered the light, rocks reflected it, the whole valley seemed resonant. Day had come to the Range of Light.

After a breakfast of bread, I again followed the Tuolumne, then crossed it on a self-operated ferry—a short board rigged to pulleys and an overhead rope. I pushed upcanyon through a steady series of switchbacks that would bring me 3,000 feet above the river. Even the heady perfume of mountain azaleas could not reverse the gnawing depression that comes with slopes that rise and rise and never seem to crest. At Harden Lake, a dark tarn rimmed with pines and aspen and grassy banks, I took the luxury of a cooling swim.

The pool's algae-covered bottom soothed hike-weary feet. I sun-dried on a flat granite slab, watching dragonflies play tag on the reeds. Butterflies as blue as the sky made their rounds among the flowers. If the Sierra foothills were Muir's bee pastures, this, I thought, would be his butterfly meadow.

I sensed the peace of which Muir wrote: "Another glorious Sierra day in which one seems to be dissolved and absorbed and sent pulsing onward we know not where. Life seems neither long nor short, and we take no more heed to save time or make haste than do the trees and stars. This is true freedom...."

A sign near the lake informed me that I had come 28.9 miles, with only 2.8 more to the roadhead. Almost 30 miles I had hiked—and yet they seemed like five. I was beginning to understand why Muir loved rambling so passionately. Without watch or odometer, what difference is there between five miles and fifty? Just don't be "time-poor," Muir would say, and rush through the glories of the Sierra without seeing them.

My brief jaunt down the Tuolumne had encompassed a wealth of glacial canyons, waterfalls, dark forests, and flowered meadows, all stirring with life. And yet this river is only a fraction of Yosemite National Park. And Yosemite, observed Muir, is but one "portion of the great Sierra loaf." The entire range—longest in the United States outside of Alaska—enfolds a tremendous amount of wild beauty. Here would Muir wander peak-to-peak for the next five years, preaching his gospel: "Going to the mountains is like going home." All youthful doubts had vanished. In the Range of Light he had found his home.

Dawn touches the jagged crest of Mount Whitney, at 14,495 feet, the loftiest peak in the 430-mile Sierra chain. Of such scenes Muir noted, "how ineffably, spiritually fine is the morning-glow on the mountaintops.... Well may the Sierra be named not the Snowy Range, but the Range of Light."

4

JOHN O' MOUNTAINS

Jumbled ridges of Washington's North Cascades shape a labyrinth of sharp spires and deep valleys called "America's Alps." Glacier Peak, at 10,568 feet, dominates a wilderness area where hikers and climbers find the exhilaration of spirit Muir experienced in mountains. In a drawing from his notebook, Muir climbs another steep peak: Yosemite's Matterhorn.

LATE ONE NIGHT in a terrible gale, a solitary and half-frozen figure danced the Highland Fling of Scotland at the top of a rockbound 14,000-foot peak in the Sierra Nevada south of Yosemite. That bizarre, puzzling figure churning the darkness was John Muir.

He was dancing not for joy—although at times he did—but for survival. Caught by the setting sun without food, fire, or even a blanket, he knew that sleep on the frigid summit would bring only death. And so he flailed and leaped and danced himself into exhaustion—and kept at it until the gray lights of dawn showed his way down.

Such misadventures never eroded Muir's love of mountains. "The Mountains are calling me and I must go," he wrote; not only the Sierra, but also the Cascades, the Olympics, the San Gabriels, and the ranges of Utah and Nevada all called to him loud and clear. From his Yosemite home, Muir set out in 1871 to explore these wilderness heights of the American West —with such determination that it seemed his legs could not be happy unless they were constantly plodding uphill. "The more savage and chilly and storm-chafed the mountains, the finer the glow on their faces," he believed. Such enthusiasm earned him the nickname "John o' Mountains."

To this connoisseur of highlands, each peak stood unique, as different as one man from another. Muir continually searched out and became familiar with individual peaks of the West, be they glacier-smoothed Sierra domes or the symmetrical volcanic cones of the Cascades. At the southern end of the Cascade Range, which rambles from northern California into British Columbia, he found a lifelong friend in Mount Shasta. Again and again he would visit this dormant volcano, a lone jolt of rock that towers nearly two miles above the California flatlands surrounding its base.

Eager to find out what attracted Muir to this mountain, I set off for Shasta's summit in the company of guide Dick Chitwood, his son Mark, and photographer David Falconer. Dick is a snow ranger with the Shasta-Trinity National Forest, which includes the mountain.

Experienced climbers find Shasta more of a long uphill walk than a true technical climb; no ropes, hardware, or advanced training are necessary. Record-setters blaze from base to summit in little more than two hours. In winter, skiers of mixed ability ply all but the top third of the mountain; it has been called the "Friendly Giant." But the unwary or unprepared have lost their lives there.

We hiked up the snowless base on a cloud-free day in August, following ski-lift stanchions. At the 9,300-foot top of the lift, Shasta briefly levels off into an altarlike brow. No icons grace this natural shrine—but we did find a guru of sorts. In the center of the ledge sat a bearded, shaggy man of indecipherable age, his legs pretzeled into the lotus position and his eyes shut tight in meditation. A bee buzzed within an inch of his nose, yet he did not flinch, apparently no more aware of that insect than of us. We continued upward. Twenty minutes later, I glanced back and found the guru still locked in meditation.

I then studied the route ahead; it was a discouraging vista of drab, lunarlike rubble left from avalanches of snow and rock. Grainy boulders of congealed lava paved steep slopes where each step forward seemed to result in slipping back three, as if we were walking up a down escalator. The tough, slippery lava chunks are so sharp and glasslike that one pierced a previous climber's hand and "took out a hunk of flesh just like it was a piece of pie," Dick recalled. The mountaineer's hand had to be amputated—a disquieting reminder that a climb of Mount Shasta is not the easy, danger-free walk that many veterans of this peak contend.

As we climbed higher, Dick suddenly shouted, "Rock! Rock! ROCK!" I looked up quickly to see a bounding boulder caroming downhill straight at us. We dodged aside—and watched it smash the spot where Dick had stood only seconds before. He was shaken.

"The mountain's moving all the time," he said with a shake of his head, adding that 40 years ago slides of rock and mud had crossed McCloud Highway—more than ten miles away. "Rocks still clatter down, but you usually just hear them."

Later, we would hear the ominous rumblings of unseen rockslides—eerie, faraway sounds that made me wonder if the mountain was rending itself in two. But no such cataclysm followed—only more rumbles that slowly crescendoed and then echoed away into silence.

From a distance, a mountain like Shasta seems eternal, immune to change. Its steepness and crumbling texture, however, rank it among the most tenuous of environments. As we plodded up to the Red Banks—huge red slabs of lava set in a curving row like giant molars—heavy fractures in the rock became increasingly apparent, foretelling more rockslides. Winds and the chuckling headwaters of the Sacramento River promised continued erosion.

We left the Red Banks and started up a snowbound trough called The Chute, and I found myself unexpectedly breaking trail. When Dick veered off to check on climbers attempting a slightly different route, I headed to his left, deciding on a more direct ascent. Slowly, laboriously, I slogged through the soft, steepening snow, sinking at times to my hips. The slope seemed almost vertical.

Still, it was a shortcut, and I was determined to make it this way—until the ledge of snow beneath me exploded into a blizzard as both my feet broke through. Suddenly I was parallel to The Chute's steep wall, sliding downhill like a runaway ski. I jammed my ice ax into the snow, but it failed to slow me. Jagged rocks from the Red Banks lay directly below — to hit them could mean disaster. I rolled over and, with all my strength, again dug in with ax and crampons. Gradually my slide stalled and finally, slowly, I stopped.

I looked up, my heart still pounding, and traced the 300-foot-long rut of my fall. A glimpse at the trail map later showed that perhaps I was not the first to fail here; the face I had attempted was labeled, aptly, "Don't Climb."

During a late lunch, we decided we had undergone enough for one day. Dick selected a campsite at the base of Misery Hill, where a couple of icy-cold pools no larger than a living room glittered with shimmering, crystalline water. As the evening sun coasted below the horizon, a blue haze flooded the lowlands. Above, subtle bands of pink and rose ringed Shasta's peak with a radiant halo.

Next morning, frost sheathed our sleeping bags as Shasta made its own weather; clouds tumbled up the mountainside in a race to the summit. Soon the day began to clear, and we started off, attacking the rocky cone known as Misery Hill.

The loose lava of this natural slag heap is usually wearisome to climb, like sand on a dune. But the frost had cemented the lava into fairly solid footing. Before long, we reached the top of Misery Hill — and gained a clear view of the summit. I felt a swell of relief that the worst had passed. Another hour and we were atop Shasta, 14,162 feet high, with nothing but the dome of the sky above us. Sunlight bathed us with warmth as nonstop winds raged, strangely, in perfect silence.

Muir noted similar daytime winds nearly a century ago. He also spent a night near the summit, though against his will. With guide Jerome Fay, he had scaled Shasta to make barometric observations for the U. S. Coast and Geodetic Survey. Ignoring menacing clouds, Muir hurried to finish his measurements. By the time they ended their work an "inconceivably violent" storm had engulfed them: "The thermometer fell 22° in a few minutes, and soon dropped below zero. The hail gave place to snow. . . . The wind . . . boomed and surged amid the desolate crags; lightning-flashes in quick succession cut the gloomy darkness. . . ." They quickly set out along a dangerous ridge to a spot where they could begin their descent.

But a thickening blizzard barred the way down; "how lavishly the snow fell only mountaineers may know," Muir wrote. He wanted to charge on, but Fay refused, preferring to remain on the mountain, despite their lack of blankets, food, tents, and firewood. They could warm themselves, said Fay, at the scalding fumaroles of the Hot Springs just below the summit. Unwilling to desert his companion, Muir remained, and the pair wallowed away the night in hot mud, the steamy jets broiling their undersides while their topsides froze in the night air.

Aware that the gas vents gave forth poisonous carbonic acid which could cause numbing sleep and death, each man kept shouting the other awake as the mercury dropped. "The weary hours wore away like dim half-forgotten years...," observed Muir. An eternity of darkness passed before the first ragged rays of dawn brought the barest relief. "Frozen, blistered, famished, benumbed... all dead but the eyes," the two rose and stumbled their way down the mountain. Muir's arm remained inert with cold; his sorely frostbitten feet never fully recovered. Injuries inflicted on Shasta would prevent him from climbing in the Alps some 20 years later.

But even while enduring severe physical pain, Muir held fast to nature's grandeur. Stars viewed during the awful night seemed to him "blessed immortals of light." Violets and larkspur blooming along the trail soothed his descent. Recuperating in a house near Shasta, he looked out his bedroom window at the "full and radiant" mountain scene, and all tortures of the stormy night "vanished like a dream."

That he survived at all was a wonder to me. Of five people we met on the summit, two had rested briefly near—not in— the Hot Springs and had lost the seats of their pants to prove it; the corrosive fumes had dissolved their dungarees. They also complained bitterly about breathing the acidy air emanating from the springs.

Despite his disastrous night atop Shasta, John o' Mountains continued to climb. But not even he kept to the mountaintops *all* the time.

His wanderings among the Cascades took him throughout the Northwest, especially Oregon, "a grand, hearty, wholesome, foodful wilderness" of bold contrasts. "Side by side there is drouth on a grand scale and overflowing moisture; flinty, sharply cut lava-beds... and smooth, flowery lawns... forests seemingly boundless and plains with no trees in sight...." I found the Cascades and Oregon equally fascinating. The mountains rise up like a wall, forcing wet breezes from the Pacific Ocean to loose all their moisture on the western part of the state, leaving the eastern portion in a dry rain shadow where annual precipitation, reported Muir, totals "only from about five to fifteen inches." Despite such dryness, he found Oregon "well supplied with rivers."

A Muir favorite was the north-flowing Deschutes River, "a large, boisterous stream, draining the eastern slope of the Cascade Range for nearly two hundred miles.... It enters the Columbia with a grand roar of falls and rapids, and at times seems almost to rival the main stream in the volume of water it carries." Named Rivière des Chutes—river of falls—by French explorers, this tumbling, white-water stream "well deserves its name," vouched Muir. Even today, it retains much of its free-running personality, and (Continued on page 118)

"...the most majestic solitary mountain I had

ver beheld."

Mount Rainier in Washington dazzled Muir when he climbed its icy slopes in 1888. "Out of the forest at last there stood the mountain, wholly unveiled, awful in bulk and majesty, filling all the view like a separate, newborn world...."

"A brave, sturdy, shaggy mountaineer of an animal, enjoying the freedom and security of crumbling ridges and overhanging cliffs. . . ." wrote Muir of the mountain goat. He sketched this long-haired, bearded animal on "the highest mountains of the Cascade Range" where it "roams in comparative security, few . . . enemies caring . . . to hunt on ground so high and so dangerous." At right, a goat browses on wild flowers near the top of Mount Angeles in Olympic National Park, Washington. Muir observed that on ice and snow, wild goats traveled "in single file guided by an old experienced leader, like a party of climbers on the Alps."

Like tiny bells, nodding pinedrops (opposite) cascade from tall red stems deep in the forests of Olympic National Park. Early-morning sun touches a highland meadow at left in the mountains of Washington. This "flowery zone of marvelous beauty" delighted Muir, prompting him to muse that nature tries "to see how many of her bright-eyed darlings she can get together in one mountain wreath." On an upper slope, a bright nosegay of onions springs from among the rocks.

it is being considered for inclusion as a National Wild and Scenic River: Its banks would then remain undeveloped.

For a look at the Deschutes River, David Falconer and I joined veteran river-runners Cal Elshoff and Walt Wolfe in their McKenzie riverboats—stubby, overgrown craft so high-prowed that both ends ride well out of the water. Passengers sit forward; oars amidships enable easy steerage. The wide beam gives each boat the totally unseaworthy look of a washtub with flippers. But they are rugged and dependable.

So, I found, were the river guides. Walt is a big man with the strength of a defensive lineman, while Cal is lanky, mustached, and partial to a pipe and, occasionally, to snuff. Deep creases etch his leathery face.

We set out near the town of Bend, in central Oregon, the river ushering us quickly through a bleak section of land. Rocky, protruding buttes and sage-dotted talus slopes alternated with lava outcroppings that pushed through the gray-green covering of juniper and sagebrush.

"Used to be nothing but grass up to the stirrups," Cal mused. "The whole region's been overgrazed. Don't see much bunchgrass any more—just sage."

Eastern Oregon's dry, crushing heat made me doubt that the volcanoes which spawned the Cascade Range had really died out. Jagged lava palisades lining the river seemed almost new; the summer sun can heat their surfaces to 180 degrees, Walt said. But even there, life—in the form of crusty green lichens—endures.

"Got any more orange drink?" I asked with dusty throat.

"Ten thousand gallons a second," Cal replied as he dipped gritty but sweet Deschutes water into a jug and added the dehydrated mix. Somehow the river stays cold in this parched land. We put ashore, leaving the sauna-like heat of the boats for a bracing plunge in the icy Deschutes.

I switched boats after our swim, joining Walt for the assault on Whitehorse—a three-mile stretch of gushing rapids. We dropped about 30 feet in the first 300 yards—nothing to rival Niagara, of course, but a respectable chute with hundreds of tiny whirlpools spurting up from the hard lava bottom. "The main thing is to keep the boat straight," Walt yelled as we set off through the noisy tangle of foam.

I heard what I thought was the hull scraping rock. I looked back at Walt and saw that an oar had snapped like a toothpick. We scrambled to replace it with a spare as the boat careered about in the current like a barrel, out of control and totally at the river's mercy.

Luckily, the Deschutes allowed us to pass unscathed. Around the next bend, however, we passed the hulk of an unluckier riverboat, nailed to a boulder by the force of the current—proof that Whitehorse is not always lenient.

With sunset's amber, nighthawks and cliff swallows massed along the river in their evening flights. A breeze promised relief from the day's heat and stuffiness. We stopped to make camp. Out came Cal's "jaffling irons"—miniature ovens that resembled long-handled, hinged hamburger molds. Heeding Cal's instructions, we lined each concave half with a slice of buttered bread and topped it with cheese, tomato sauce, and meat; we then closed the irons and shoved them into the fire. After a few minutes, we had tartlike hot sandwiches that he called jaffled pizza. Later, we followed the same procedure and made blueberry pie. I found jaffled food not only tasty and filling, but also exceptionally easy to prepare. The irons—which Cal purchased in Australia—also eliminate the need for cookpots, utensils, and plates.

Our second day on the Deschutes dawned with jaffled eggs and bacon. After breakfast, I headed to the river with a fly rod. The early hour and my own inexperience combined to make for a morning of subtle challenges: first, choosing and tying on a fly, then aiming for that quiet spot where a big one just jumped —and turning around to see my line hopelessly snagged in some weeds. Cast followed cast, and with each came a new flick of the wrist, a change of flies, a different target—but no fish. I recalled another dawn many years before, the first time my father took me to the wilderness. I hooked my first rainbow trout and fried it for breakfast, after sleeping out under the stars and listening all night to the rippling creek. Warm memories of that past vacation flooded my consciousness. The quiet beauty, the smell of woodsmoke, that glorious sunrise of the past merged with present pleasures. I reeled in the limp fishline and returned to camp—empty-handed but not at all unhappy.

THOUGH MUIR WAS NO FISHERMAN, the fish themselves delighted him. Gigantic runs of salmon up the Columbia River— "one of the chief attractions of the Pacific Coast"—fascinated him with brawling fish "twenty to eighty pounds each, plump and smooth like loaves of bread ready for the oven." So plentiful were the salmon that Indians burned them as fuel and settlers fertilized their crops with them. "Used, wasted, canned and sent in shiploads to all the world, a grand harvest was reaped every year while nobody sowed," decried Muir. Even in his day this long-abundant crop had begun to fail, and the government restocked the rivers of the Northwest with millions of fry each year. A planned program of restocking continues today.

Despite changes brought by dams and man-made lakes, the Columbia remains a mountain river. Spawned in the Canadian Rockies, it flows south and then west, severing the Cascade and Coast Ranges on its course to the Pacific. John o' Mountains especially loved its highland gorges and waterfalls, but like salmon and the river itself, he somehow would find himself at sea level, drawn by the intense variety of the grand Pacific coast. "A scramble along the Oregon sea-bluffs proves as richly exciting to lovers of wild beauty as heart could wish. Here are three hundred miles of pictures of rock and water...," he exclaimed. The varied coastline holds salt marshes, sea stacks, heaps of lava, and graceful sand dunes, all within just a few miles of each other. The one constant is the sea itself.

"No calm comes to these shores," Muir noted. "The rocks, glistening in sunshine and foam, are never wholly dry.... How grand the songs of the waves about them, every wave a fine, hearty storm...taking its rise on the breezy plains of the sea, perhaps thousands of miles away."

The best way to see the Oregon coast, I quickly discovered, is Muir's way—alone. To ramble the undulating beaches in the solitude of nature is to know the elements—earth and water and air. It is to unwind, to rediscover thoughts long forgotten, to feel the contentment of being alone without being lonely. The cold, briny winds hitting me square in the face made me feel dynamically alive.

Just south of Cape Foulweather, the churning sea has sculpted sandstone cliffs into caves and pits; one I liked was the cavernous Devil's Punch Bowl. Inrushing waters at high tide crash and sprawl up its walls, spouting out a hole on top. At low tide, winds take over the chore of erosion.

The wind proved its force to me one night atop a bluff near the Punch Bowl. I went to sleep after watching the sunset glow, then turn to gloom, and burn out—only to wake a few hours later in the raging center of a sandstorm! Sand from all directions pelted me with millions of punches infinitesimal in size but infinite in combined fury. No wonder the cliffs erode so fast, I thought, in the midst of this maelstrom. I could only keep my eyes tightly shut and grumble about Muir's blind love for Oregon's "dark, stormy nights, when, crouching in some hollow on the top of some jutting headland, we may gaze and listen undisturbed in the heart of it."

I felt anything but undisturbed. By dawn, the wind had stopped and I gingerly arose. Sand filled my ears and nose, caked my eyelids, and had worked its way into every crevice of flesh and clothing. I brushed off what I could, packed up, and continued my walk.

A beautiful desolation enfolded the Oregon coast that morning; eroded sandstone bluffs seemed especially forlorn amid the crashing waves. Giant gray driftwood logs lay just out of the surf's reach, bleached and worn like so many dinosaur bones. Yet less than a mile up the coast, miniature fiords, estuaries, and basins etched the lava beach with intricate tidal pools filled with life. Countless seaweeds flourished; mussels and barnacles, cemented shell to shell, completely covered the rock. Jade-colored sea anemones six inches wide resembled shaggy shrubs.

The incoming tide surged through labyrinthine channels, slammed into rocky walls, and doubled back, churning itself into froth as it constantly reshaped the pools and flooded them with cold but nourishing water.

Just inland from what he called the sea's "grand, savage harmony," John o' Mountains relished the "one vast, evenly planted forest" blanketing western Oregon and Washington. The "whole country is solemnly soaked and poulticed with the gray, streaming clouds and fogs, night and day, with marvelous constancy," Muir reported of this region during the cold months. The richness of this land attracted farmers, always busy with "chopping, girdling, and burning the edge of the encircling forest . . . regarding the trees as their greatest enemies—a sort of larger pernicious weed immensely difficult to get rid of." Muir chided his fellow Americans for plundering their evergreen treasures—just to make farmland and to feed the dozens of sawmills on Puget Sound. Though he admitted such mills were nearly invisible in the vast and "almost entirely virgin" land, he had the foresight even then to warn against "this fierce storm of steel that is devouring the forests." He pleaded that some virgin woods "might be spared to the world, not as dead lumber, but as living trees."

Decades later, a huge expanse of forested wilderness was preserved by the creation of Olympic National Park—nearly 900,000 acres of mountains, wild Pacific shore, and dense rain forest on Washington's Olympic Peninsula. The astounding profusion of plants in its rain forests especially captivated the botanist in Muir: ". . . in the untrodden woods where no axe has been lifted, where a deep, rich carpet of brown and golden mosses covers all the ground like a garment, pressing warmly about the feet of the trees and rising in thick folds softly and kindly over every fallen trunk, leaving no spot naked or uncared-for, there the rain is welcomed, and every drop that falls finds a place and use as sweet and pure as itself."

One such plant haven is the Queets River valley, which probes westward from the Olympic Mountains to the ocean. Here I saw, as Muir did, a few open meadows of bright-hued wild flowers. But this valley is primarily dense rain forest, and the color that predominates is green—from the thick forest canopy to the fern-draped floor. Yet the forest is no dull monotone. A hundred shades of green abound: sun-drenched treetops, blackish-green trunks strewn with chartreuse mosses, emerald ferns and shamrocklike oxalis. Eerie, leaf-filtered green light flows everywhere. Billowy club moss beards the trees like century-old cobwebs. A damp earthy smell fills the air, and the silence seems all-encompassing.

The silence, however, was only temporary. Sudden loud chirpings and whistlings sounded overhead. I scanned the trees to see what birds made such unfamiliar calls. The noisemakers were not feathered, however, but small and furry.

Three Douglas squirrels romped up and down a hemlock, their back-and-forth chorus of chatter sounding melodic. Named for David Douglas, a botanist from Scotland who rambled through the Northwest half a century before Muir did, these playful midgets have large, fluffy tails that arch gracefully over their heads.

Muir enjoyed these squirrels; often they provided his sole companionship and entertainment on long hikes through the mountains. He dubbed the Douglas "squirrel of squirrels . . . crisp and glossy and sound as a sunbeam," noting that "though only a few inches long, so intense is his fiery vigor and restlessness, he . . . makes himself more important than the great bears that shuffle through the berry tangles beneath him. . . . One never tires of this bright spark of life, the brave little voice crying in the wilderness."

WANDERING FARTHER up the Queets valley, I met Merle Meinicke, a seasonal Park ranger who proudly led me to one of the Park's largest trees — a Sitka spruce. A ten-minute walk along a forest path brought us to it, some 200 vertical feet of tree. "That's after it was topped by lightning," Merle added. Six feet above the ground, the trunk measured more than 42 feet in circumference.

The Park also boasts the world's largest known Douglas fir, a species named for the Scottish botanist. "The finest building material anywhere," Merle explained. "It's the tree that built the Northwest." Such giants fill much of Olympic National Park's rain forest, which contains several world champions — each the largest known tree of its species.

Many smaller trunks, I noticed, started four or five feet above the forest floor, standing tiptoe on roots that seem to have grown too high up. Merle explained: "Sure sign of a nurse log. See that dead spruce?" He pointed to a fallen giant speckled by dozens of small hemlock saplings drawing nourishment from its decay. "Young trees grow fast on them, but their roots can't go through the nurse, so they straddle it. When the nurse log finally rots away, the living trees are left all alone, high off the ground. A big wind might come along and blow them down." And then the nurse-sapling cycle begins again.

Occasional gaps — caused perhaps by fallen trees — puncture the close green canopy of the valley, affording glimpses of the grand Olympic Mountains. John o' Mountains was quick to note such views and observed: "Ambitious climbers, seeking

". . . to test their strength and skill . . . push on to the summit of Mount Olympus," high point of the peninsula. "But the grandest excursion of all to be made hereabouts is to Mount Rainier, to climb to the top of its icy crown."

In 1888, Muir scaled Rainier from the south; today most climbers follow a similar route up this singular crag guarding the western edge of the Cascades. "Did not mean to climb it," Muir jotted afterward, "but got excited and soon was on top." Well, perhaps. He set out, however, not on an impromptu walk but with a well-organized 12-man expedition, complete with packhorses and "a cumbersome abundance of campstools and blankets." They reached timberline at a stunning vantage point now called Alta Vista—high view.

"Out of the forest at last there stood the mountain," Muir recorded, "wholly unveiled, awful in bulk and majesty, filling all the view like a separate, newborn world, yet withal so fine and so beautiful it might well fire the dullest observer to desperate enthusiasm. Long we gazed in silent admiration, buried in tall daisies and anemones by the side of a snowbank." The following day they climbed to the 10,000-foot level, making camp between the Nisqually and Cowlitz Glaciers. One member of that climbing party named the site Camp Muir.

Camp Muir still stands today at 10,000 feet, serving as a way station for summit-bound hikers. "It's the only reasonable place to camp at that elevation—so it's probably where Muir was," said Jim Tobin, superintendent of Mount Rainier National Park. Other sites, he explained, are too precarious, windswept, or full of glaciers and crevasses.

Almost all climbers stay overnight at Camp Muir because the summit climb is too rugged to make in a single day from the usual starting point—the Park's visitor center at Paradise, named for the heavenly, flower-filled meadows nearby. When I arrived at Paradise, it lay mittened in a damp fog. Wet, whiskery needles of snowbound hemlocks nuzzled me as I poked about the woods. The slumped top of Rainier, veiled in drizzly gray mist, reminded me of a big white sleeping bear.

Within a few hours, however, the mists began to clear, revealing the glory of Rainier—all but the very top, where a puffy beret of clouds sat jauntily, refusing to run away from the now-burning sun. Along with others, I decided to climb to Camp Muir despite the report of one bedraggled mountaineer who told of hail and lightning the previous night. But the sun was cheery, and lofty Rainier too inviting for me to turn back.

I set out at four in the afternoon with new friends I had met at Paradise—Erich and Debbie, in team with Bridgette, a Labrador retriever. "She's a better climber than I am," said Debbie. But talented or not, Bridgette could not scale Rainier—Park rules bar pets from making the ascent, a ranger warned. The trio sadly returned to Paradise. I went (Continued on page 128)

"...a deep, rich carpet of...mosses covers all the ground like a garment...leaving no spot naked or uncared-for...."

Tangle of roots flares from the trunk of a hemlock in a lush rain forest near the sea coast in Olympic National Park. Cloverlike wood sorrel creeps up the tree's moss-matted trunk. A thick cover of ferns and vines (above) cushions the floor of such rain forests. Dense ocean fogs and frequent storms sweep the western part of the Olympic Peninsula, producing these rich oases of green.

Isolated rock pinnacle, a sea stack stands sentinel at low tide along the
Pacific coast of Olympic National Park. Many of these jutting rocks—
remnants of a surf-battered coastline long since washed into the sea—
remain connected to the shore by sandspits during low tide. Muir described
the power of the ocean: "...massive waves...get close to the bluffs ere
they break, and the thundering shock shakes the rocks to their foundations." As the tide recedes, a small pool (opposite, top) captures sea water
and becomes a sanctuary for sea life. Jellyfish the size of marbles (opposite,
bottom) shimmer on the sand after a wave has left them stranded.

on alone, with a lowering sun and about five snowy, uphill miles to go.

Soon I was up and out of the trees. South of me, distant Mount Adams and Mount St. Helens of the Cascade Range looked like islands afloat in the sky, lapped by frothy waves of cloud. Similar clouds, I discovered with a start, were beginning to lap at me. Chased by them and lured by Rainier's still-gleaming dome, I hurriedly resumed climbing toward Camp Muir.

The snow grew mushier, and I grew to dread the inevitable plunge with each step. All I could do was sink, pull out the submerged leg, plant it ahead of the other, and sink again in laborious repetition. Golden marmots perched on nearby rocks called out in piercing whistles that sounded to me like jeering laughter at my struggling plight.

Farther on, marmot whistles gave way to more serious sounds—deep crackles and bangs as the Nisqually and Cowlitz Glaciers slowly shifted their massive bulks. At 6 p.m. I passed a sign indicating I had come only 2.2 miles from Paradise. I was less than halfway to Camp Muir, and two hours were already gone—along with much of my energy. The clouds caught up with me, and rain began to fall, although Rainier stayed in the sunlight. I paused to pull on a sweater and poncho, and turned my back to the wind. But just as suddenly as it had appeared, the cloud cover blew away—and Rainier stood majestic, completely unveiled for the first time. The rain, however, had erased part of the trail; the path that had begun at Paradise as a bulldozer-size slash through the snow had narrowed to a single set of footprints—my own. I could see no other person above or below, just the overwhelming mass of Mount Rainier. Fluffy ribbons of clouds traced across the sky and began to pinken, a reminder that I had better quicken my pace if I hoped to make Camp Muir before dark.

The sun soon set. I had perhaps 45 minutes of afterglow to see my way to camp. But still I could not ignore the magic light as it painted each cloud a different shade. One always outshone the others, clinging to the pinks and deep reds just a little longer, seeming to draw the sun into itself and radiate it outward—while all its puffy companions turned to purple and gray, and then died.

Even the purples and grays were gone when I finally reached Camp Muir—at 9:32 p.m., more than five hours after setting out. I had barely enough light to find a place to sleep. Camp Muir—a collection of wood and stone huts—seemed deserted; all was quiet, all asleep. The climbers had missed the display of clouds, storms, sunset, and alpenglow. But for good reason: Most would arise by 2 a.m. to attempt the summit.

I made my bed outside, without tent, stove, or fire. Muir's night there was also fireless, and I suppose I felt a bit of kinship with John o' Mountains. Even today, amid the 5,500 climbers who ascend Rainier each year, it is still possible to be alone with the mountain, to sleep out in the wind and climb with only bare essentials—ice ax, crampons, and good boots. Luckily the weather held through the night, and roughing it on Rainier was not rough at all—I had dinner in bed while the lights of Paradise twinkled below. I soon drifted into the deep sleep of the mountaineer. A bright quarter-moon rose at about 1:30 in the morning, its rich golden slice of light jolting me awake. It prompted a guide, also awakened by the radiance, to comment that he had "never, ever seen it that bright."

Rainier's night sky set off the moon with a huge, unpolluted blackness. The sky was peppered with the bright pinpoints of stars. Shooting stars traced their quickly-dying paths as guides roused their charges, roped them together, and shuffled off, clanking and huffing like a pack train. I returned to sleep. Not everyone had left yet, and I hoped to tie in with a later party.

I awoke to find Rainier again overcast—and all climbers gone. Determined to catch up with some, I set out at 4:30, crossed the stable Cowlitz Glacier—one of two dozen ice rivers coursing Rainier—and scaled shattered Cathedral Rocks to see the sun rise, a glowing red ball sandwiched between clouds and the black, tortured crag of Little Tahoma Peak.

Beyond Cathedral Rocks lay the cracked surface of Ingraham Glacier. Here, street-wide crevasses fissure the ice, meeting in central points like starfish. Muir noted such dangers nearly 90 years ago, warning of Rainier's "network of yawning crevasses, outspread like lines of defense against any attempt to win the summit."

These moody chasms swell and shrink with the weather, and can run thousands of feet deep. They are a major risk that one must accept in climbing mountains like Rainier. Gigantic ice chunks as large as the stones of the Great Pyramid lay jumbled about; platoons of huge icicles covered the few thrusts of bare rock. The beauty that I was discovering on the way to the top was becoming my reason for climbing—more than the summit itself.

Ahead lay the winding trail to Disappointment Cleaver, a sharp outcropping about a mile from the mountain's crest. In some places, 45-degree slopes promised sheer toil. I trudged 30 steps and rested, then took 30 more—an endless cycle up this giant white ramp.

At about 12,000 feet, Muir's party had stopped to hammer steel caulks, a form of crampons, into their shoes. Alpenstocks —steel-pointed walking sticks—served as ice axes on the "bare, hard, snowless ice, extremely slippery." They carried rope for emergencies, but did not lash themselves together. It was later noted that the climbers "had no security other than careful placing of the feet and the support of the alpenstock."

During my climb, I relied on a similar combination of caution and good mountaineering equipment.

Nearing the snowy summit, I finally caught up with some ascending climbers—a party of five lunching before the final assault. I joined them, and sat on the rocky rim of the crater that crowns Rainier. Here, Muir noted some "sulphurous fumes ... giving out a sickening smell," but I only detected a bit of odorless steam.

We planned to go up together, but as we rested, the blue sky turned to cloud—thin, uncertain shreds that sped across the sky, massing and drawing apart. My newfound friends voted to head down. Did I wish to go with them?

Well, yes. But the topmost summit lay within view, less than a quarter-mile away, free of crevasses and steep slopes. Rifts in the cloud cover further encouraged me to continue my climb; the five set off downhill.

Before me lay a fairly level walk—just across a shallow crater and up a short ridge. I traversed the crater almost without effort, and after only 20 minutes stood alone on the top, a snowy pinnacle called Columbia Crest, because Rainier once was considered the highest peak in America. My uphill trek had ended. I now stood where Muir had, 14,410 feet above the oceans, and I drank in the same view he had praised.

To stand on any summit brings a surge of exaltation. But no one ever conquers a peak, I reflected; the mountain only permits a climber to pause there for a few brief moments. And yet no matter how short that stay, the impact of it never fades: Memories of my Rainier climb still jostle their way to the forefront of my mind. I cannot look at the mountain—even a postcard of it—without warmly recalling the day when Rainier and I briefly became one.

Strangely, it was this mountain's windy dome that brought the usually jubilant Muir a rare pang of loneliness. He later mused: ". . . one feels far from home so high in the sky . . . more pleasure is to be found at the foot of mountains than on their frozen tops." But with his very next words, the eagle in him returned: "Doubly happy, however, is the man to whom lofty mountain-tops are within reach, for the lights that shine there illumine all that lies below." And so, joyously, did John o' Mountains reaffirm his primal love of all highland steeps.

Glistening tidal pool along the Washington coast nurtures flowerlike sea anemones, bright starfish, and verdant surfgrass. Muir, intrigued by the Pacific shore's ruggedness, described the rocks as "marvels of wave-sculpture . . . holding the homes . . . of multitudes of seafaring animals."

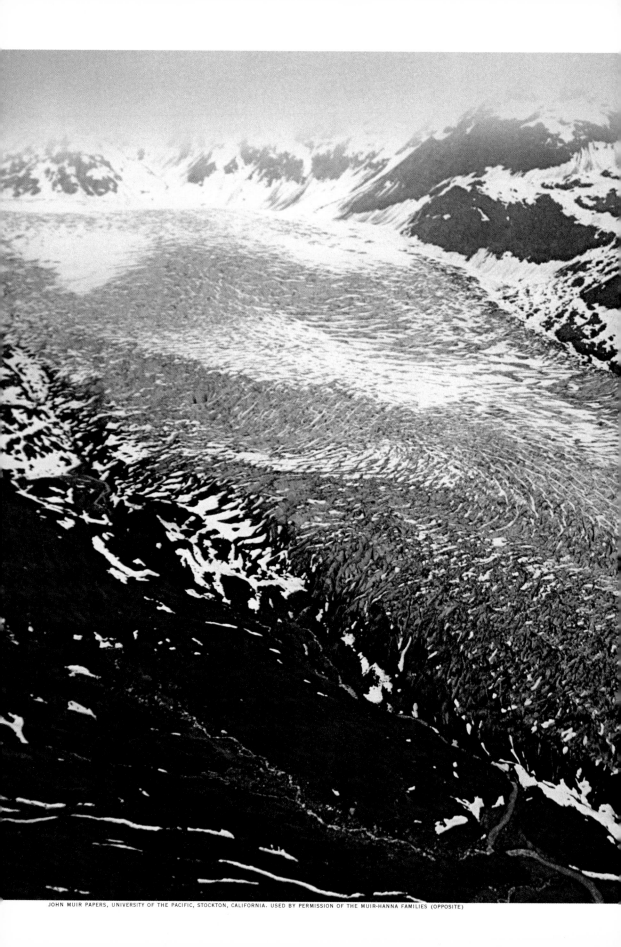

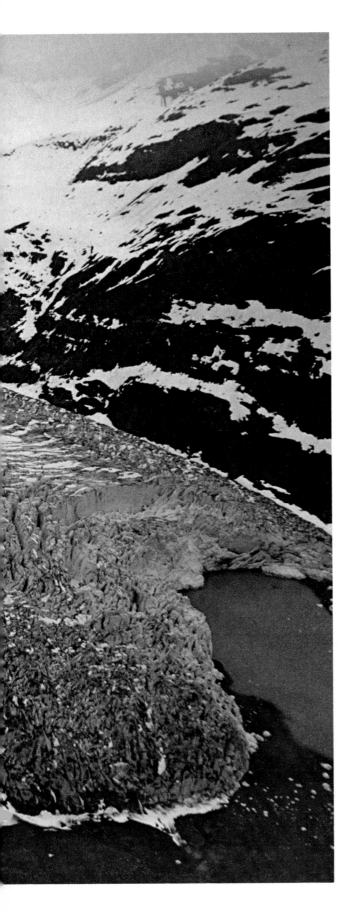

5

VOYAGES TO ALASKA

"God's crystal temple," Muir called such massive ice sheets as Reid Glacier, which stretches from mountain to salt water at Glacier Bay National Monument, Alaska. Muir first voyaged to southeastern Alaska in 1879 to explore its "noble, newborn scenery" and to help validate his glacial theories by firsthand observation of living glaciers. During his travels in Alaska, he sketched an Eskimo woman (above).

ALASKA—A SPRAWLING, ALLURING WILDERNESS far to the north—beckoned Muir with its massive glaciers, its icebound peaks, and its amazing diversity of plant and animal life. This vast, wild, and mysterious land prompted naturalist John Burroughs, a good friend of Muir, to remark with a sense of wonder: "Things are on a new scale."

On his first voyage to this primeval realm, Muir left San Francisco aboard a steamer in the summer of 1879, rejoicing over the "merry schools of porpoises, a square mile of them" that escorted his ship. Forested, wave-battered shores along the way attracted him, and he gloried in the "rolling, pitching, flying water"—while most other passengers succumbed to the agony of seasickness.

"To the lover of pure wildness Alaska is one of the most wonderful countries in the world," he chanted after his first voyage, during which he threaded among hundreds of islands off British Columbia and southeastern Alaska. Today, ferries of the state's Marine Highway System closely parallel Muir's route; photographer Farrell Grehan and I boarded just such a northbound ferry in Seattle.

Countless camelback islands, draped with western hemlock and Sitka spruce, flanked our way; as the nonstop shudder of the boat drove us northward we saw increasingly wilder slopes. Foamy white waterfalls and near-vertical streams laced some islands, uniting ever-craggier peaks with the sea. Similarly pristine sights had provoked Muir to declare, repeatedly, his desire to hop off the steamer and race up the mountains. Only the captain's refusal to put ashore prevented him from mountain climbing his way to Alaska.

Even today, this wild and sparsely inhabited country sparks excitement. My shipmates—a collection as varied as America—shared a common feeling of expectation. Sister Mary Holy Cross wondered about the Alaska homeland she had left for the convent in the 1920's, a home she would now revisit in celebration of her jubilee—"fifty years in the order." An 18-year-old trucker—packing both a hunting knife and a loaded pistol—anticipated rough-and-tumble times on his way to Ketchikan's seafood canneries. His shipboard hours passed quickly but unprofitably in all-night poker games with a young ex-dealer from the blackjack tables of Las Vegas. A soapstone carver looked forward to a peaceful life-style in Wrangell. Mountain climbers hunkered around detailed maps of Mount McKinley—its 20,320-foot summit their destination. A college co-ed envisioned a $1,000-a-month summer job. Locked together on that small ferry for three days, we all quickly became friends.

On the second day of our voyage north, I saw an astonishingly familiar face. I stared, blinked, and stared again. The eagle brows, the glacial blue eyes, the curly beard and the angular face all shouted "John Muir."

"You're not the first to point out the resemblance," Don Lennartson said with a shy grin. "I guess I do sort of look like him. But it still always surprises me when people mention it."

The similarity, I quickly discovered, transcends the physical. Don, an amateur ecologist and devotee of Muir's writings, loves to ramble in the wilderness, believing that the old wanderer "speaks to my condition. His style fulfills a need in me—I want to experience the land as he did." Don appreciates wildness—and John Muir. "Muir was fully integrated. He realized there's no reason to separate scientific knowledge and romantic beauty. That's where his genius lay."

Both beauty and science drew Muir to Alaska; the immensity of the land left him flabbergasted. Mountains, glaciers, fiords, bays—nature had wrought them all in grand proportions, making this land a "paradise of the poets, the abode of the blessed." More than anything else, John Muir loved Alaska's ice. Monstrous glaciers spilled over the roughhewn land, and they provided ready workshops where he could test and modify his glacial theories.

Like Muir, Farrell and I would climb glaciers and canoe fiords. Alaska is so large, however, and nature so spendthrift with her pleasures, that the best way we found to meet this vastness and have any chance of seeing it was by air.

Upon arriving in Wrangell—Muir's first landfall—we set out in a single-engine plane to explore nearby LeConte Glacier. From a distance, this ice field yielded a strange impression to me; I saw it as a titanic crumb cake dyed pale blue.

Quickly, though, the crumbs resolved into row after row of ice ridges hundreds of feet high; yawning clefts dropped deep into the glacier, revealing ice colored a rich cobalt blue. The blue was so intense—almost painfully so—that it seemed to bore through my closed eyelids. Muir referred to this shade as "...the most startling, chilling, almost shrieking vitriol blue...." It occurs only in the oldest, innermost parts of the glacier, where the ice is densest.

Seaward from LeConte, icebergs packed and dispersed with the tides. Many spanned several hundred feet, but even these were miniscule in comparison to the mother glacier. Seals by the hundred loitered on the ice floes, curled like commas on a sheet of paper. With just this first glimpse of Alaska's wilderness, I could fully understand why John Muir considered it "so fine, so tender, so ethereal, that all penwork seems hopelessly unavailing."

Alaska's towns, however, impressed Muir but little. Showing his habitual lack of affection for human communities, he labeled Wrangell "a rough place. No mining hamlet...I ever saw, approached it in picturesque, devil-may-care abandon." He disparaged its layout as "a lawless draggle of wooden huts and houses, built in crooked lines, wrangling around the boggy shore of the island . . . without the slightest subordination to . . . building laws of any kind."

Muir quickly left Wrangell, lured by nearby mountains. He was an individualist, and even in Alaska, a land that prides itself on individuality, Muir was singular. One night he went out in a heavy rainstorm, "anxious to see how the Alaska trees behave in storms and hear the songs they sing." On a hill over-looking the town, he nurtured a bit of burning tinder within a dead tree into "a pillar of flame thirty or forty feet high . . . casting a red glare into the flying clouds." Muir always remembered the raging bonfire "for its triumphant storm-defying grandeur, and the wondrous beauty of the psalm-singing, lichen-painted trees which it brought to light." While he was enthralled by the flames and the drenching storm, the towns-people below — able to see only the reddened clouds but not the fire — were badly frightened. Settlers feared a volcano was brewing; Indians assessed the sky as a terrible omen and fled to their missionaries for guidance.

Muir continually mystified the people of Wrangell. "What can the fellow be up to?" one resident asked. "I saw him the other day on his knees, looking at a stump as if he expected to find gold in it. He seems to have no serious object whatever."

As always, Muir was simply following the dictates of his heart, immersing himself in Alaska's wild beauty. Extensive botanical walks recalled "the cool sphagnum and carex bogs of Wisconsin and Canada," which he had wandered as a youth. "I never saw a richer bog and meadow growth anywhere," he wrote of the muskeg near Wrangell.

Muskeg — from an Algonquin Indian word meaning "grassy bog" — refers to wet, peaty tracts of undulating land; mosses and other small plants form a spongy green cushion, dappled with dark, tannin-stained pools of water. When I first explored a muskeg, I sensed only bleakness. It seemed wet and flat, a nearly treeless expanse of dull green.

But I lingered — crouching and staring — and slowly, like an abstract painting, this green sea became alive with exciting de-tails. I discovered a Lilliputian realm of valleys, lakes, and forests formed by small plants. Sundews reached out with sticky, globular fingers to snare insects; lichens, fungi, and other tiny plants speckled the earth with red, gold, and auburn — ablaze like a New England autumn. These colors contrasted with the softer hues of white dwarf dogwoods, lavender bog laurels, and pink bog rosemary. Marsh marigolds, Labrador-tea, and deep purple mosses added their color and fragrance.

In this miniature wonderland, only a few contorted pines, cedars, and spruces — no larger than saplings — rose above the moss-and-wild flower level. But one stump a mere five inches thick boasted more than 500 growth rings, even though it stood no taller than a man.

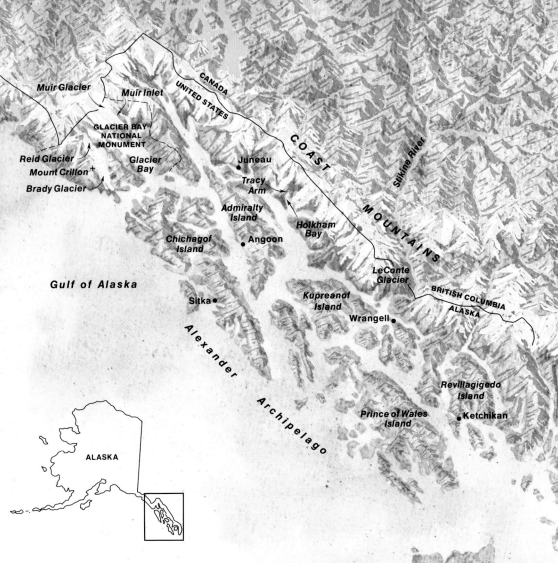

Muir Glacier

Muir Inlet

CANADA
UNITED STATES

GLACIER BAY
NATIONAL
MONUMENT

Reid Glacier
Mount Crillon +
Brady Glacier

Glacier
Bay

Juneau

Tracy
Arm

Admiralty
Island

Chichagof
Island

Angoon

Holkham
Bay

C O A S T

Stikine River

M O U N T A I N S

LeConte
Glacier

BRITISH COLUMBIA
ALASKA

Kupreanof
Island

Wrangell

Gulf of Alaska

Sitka

A l e x a n d e r

A r c h i p e l a g o

Revillagigedo
Island

Prince of Wales
Island

Ketchikan

ALASKA

Queen
Charlotte
Islands

"I have found southeastern Alaska a good,
healthy country to live in," declared Muir after
discovering that the climate had few extremes
of heat or cold. During his six excursions to
Alaska, Muir climbed, hiked, and canoed
through this rugged, glacier-carved land,
mapping waterways and sketching plants,
animals, and people. Tlingit Indians intrigued
him with tales of a "big ice-mountain bay" —
now Glacier Bay National Monument. He
paddled there with a friend, missionary S. Hall
Young, and explored its tidewater glaciers —
one of which now bears Muir's name. In
Alaska, Muir continually sought to experience
the great forces of nature; he once climbed a
mountain in a blinding snowstorm, provoking
an Indian companion to remark, "Muir must
be a witch to seek knowledge in such a place
. . . and in such miserable weather."

137

It's a wonder the trees grow at all. Muskegs trap water like sponges, breeding an undernourished, liquid, peaty soil too acidic for most trees. The acidity retards not only growth but also decay, for it bathes all muskeg plants in a natural pickling solution that shields them from the oxygen necessary for decomposition. Past generations die but never seem to rot; each year, a new layer adds its thickness to the boggy foundation. Some muskegs have peat moss dozens of feet thick.

Just as Wrangell's muskegs brought Muir many new plant friends, Wrangell itself fostered some memorable human companionships. The day of Muir's arrival, local Presbyterian missionary S. Hall Young met his boat to welcome its load of high-ranking church officials. Young was struck by the intense appearance of "a lean, sinewy man of forty" on board, his "peering blue eyes already eagerly scanning the islands and mountains." Soon he met "Professor Muir, the Naturalist." Muir and Young became lifelong friends, master and disciple always ready to trek the wilds of Alaska together.

Once, they and the visiting churchmen churned up the nearby Stikine River in a steamer. When a gale idled the boat 150 miles upriver, the captain directed his passengers to "Amuse yourselves." Muir grabbed some hardtack, and he and Young set off for a nearby mountain. Though he had known Muir only a few days, Young had already caught his wilderness fever. In a memoir written years later, Young recounted: "What a matchless climate! What sweet, lung-filling air! Sunshine that had no weakness in it—as if we were springing plants. Our sinews like steel springs, muscles like India rubber, feet soled with iron to grip the rocks. Ten miles? Eight thousand feet? Why, I felt equal to forty miles and the Matterhorn!"

Muir, already twitching with the excitement of another climb, "went wild" when they discovered a fairyland of delicate blossoms part way up the peak. Young observed that, "From cluster to cluster of flowers he ran, falling on his knees, babbling in unknown tongues, prattling a curious mixture of scientific lingo and baby talk." With "boyish enthusiasm" he stuffed his pockets and shirt full of flowers—and soon appropriated Young's pockets as well, planning to continue his studies aboard the steamer.

The two climbers dallied long among the flowers, until the approaching "jewel of the day"—as Young called sunset—impelled Muir to try and reach the summit in time for sundown.

"Muir began to *slide* up that mountain," wrote his companion. "Eye, hand and foot all connected dynamically; with no appearance of weight to his body. . . ." Young had climbed before, but never with such an accomplished adventurer, whose "movements were almost like flying, legs and arms moving with perfect precision and unfailing judgement." Had the missionary been alone, the steepening trail would have forced a quick retreat. "But Muir was my 'control' ... and I never thought of doing anything else but following him."

The sun was descending rapidly when they began their final sprint to the summit, Muir intent on seeing the horizon before the glowing red ball dropped from view. Young followed as best he could — until a loose stone gave way underfoot and he plummeted down a narrow, rocky cleft. Striking out with his arms to either side of the gorge, he dislocated both shoulders; he hit bottom, then slid down toward another precipice, vainly trying to dig in with toes and chin. He came to rest on a small ledge deep within the rock cleft, helpless and in agony: "I still felt myself slipping, slipping down the greasy slate," he recalled. Tortured by the pain in his shoulders and the fear of falling, he gave an involuntary shudder — and slid yet another inch toward the abyss. Already, his feet hung over the edge. Muir speedily responded, whistling a few Scotch airs as he probed his way down the rock face toward Young. "I felt a careful hand on my back, fumbling with the waistband of my pants, my vest and shirt, gathering all in a firm grip. ... 'Now!' he said, and I slid out of the cleft with a rattling shower of stones and gravel. My head swung down, my impotent arms dangling, and I stared straight at the glacier, a thousand feet below. Then my feet came against the cliff. 'Work downwards with your feet.' I obeyed." Step by step, Muir aided the helpless Young out of peril. They had to climb up as well as down; when one rocky wall grew so slick that Muir needed both hands to scale it, he grabbed Young's collar in his *teeth!* He steadily clawed up the sheer face despite his burden. "How he did it, I know not," Young wrote later. "The miracle grows as I ponder it. The wall was almost perpendicular and smooth. My weight on his jaws dragged him outwards. ... It was utterly impossible, yet he did it!"

"A picture of icy wildness unspeakably pure and sublime," wrote Muir of Alaska's glacier-clad landscape. In this sketch, moraines— earth pushed up by moving ice—trace lines on Reid Glacier.

After trying to reset both of Young's shoulders but succeeding with only one, Muir continued down the mountain with his companion, easing him down sheer walls and around glacial crevasses in deepening darkness.

The descent progressed with agonizing slowness. But Muir remained "always cheery, full of talk and anecdote, cracking jokes with me, infusing me with his own indomitable spirit. He was eyes, hands, feet, and heart to me." They straggled back to the steamboat at 7:30 a.m.—almost 18 hours after leaving on what was supposed to have been an afternoon jaunt.

Excruciating attempts to reset Young's shoulder bones ensued. "They went at it with two men pulling at the towel knotted about my wrist, two others pulling against them, foot braced to foot, Muir manipulating my shoulder with his sinewy hands, and the stocky Captain, strong and compact as a bear, with his heel against the yarn ball in my armpit, takes me by the elbow and says, 'I'll set it or pull the arm off!'"

Luckily for Young, the arm was set, but only after a battle of a couple of hours; whiskey deadened his pain. And yet of this hellish experience, Young held only "one overpowering regret." Unlike John Muir, who later returned to climb that mountain, he "never saw the sunset from that peak." Young, converted by Muir, had already become a fanatic lover of wilderness.

Though Young's mountaintop accident forced him to avoid steep climbs thereafter, he accompanied Muir on many lowland excursions, becoming his constant Alaska traveling companion. They made a good team—Young, the devoted missionary in search of new people to convert; Muir, eager to explore wilderness. The most reliable charts they had of southeastern Alaska dated to Captain George Vancouver's hurried explorations in 1794, when ice had covered much of the land. But this deterred neither Muir nor Young; they would set off in a canoe of red cedar, manned by four Tlingit Indians, and make their own maps where Vancouver's failed.

"We are going to write some history, my boy," Muir counseled Young. "Hurry! We are daily losing the most important news of all the world." To Muir, of course, that news was glacial, not journalistic.

And so began a six-week trip through the islands north of Wrangell, where "every hour was new and strange," wrote Young. At Sum Dum Bay—now Holkham Bay south of Juneau—they tried to explore a two-pronged fiord slashing the mainland. Muir called this a "wild unfinished Yosemite.... No ice-work that I have ever seen surpasses this." But icebergs charged "down upon us like an army," Young noted, "spread-

Ice ax in hand, John Muir leads S. Hall Young's dog Stickeen across the jagged ice of Brady Glacier in Glacier Bay. To protect his companion's paws from the shredding sharpness of the ice, Muir fashioned moccasins from his handkerchief. Stickeen adopted Muir during his visit to Alaska in 1880, and for four months he accompanied him everywhere; Muir later wrote a children's book about their adventures together. "I have known many dogs," he reflected, "and many a story I could tell of their wisdom and devotion; but to none do I owe so much as to Stickeen."

ing out in loose formation and then gathering into a barrier"
and forcing their retreat—a retreat that would continue to nag
at Muir for many months.

Mysterious tales of a treeless, "big ice-mountain bay"—
a region that even Indians rarely visited—then lured them
farther north, despite the approach of winter. Late in October
they reached their goal—"a picture of icy wildness unspeakably pure and sublime," wrote Muir. It was a narrow inlet—
later named Glacier Bay and made a national monument
—running in from the coast some 45 miles. Eight active glaciers
spilled into it. Vancouver's charts stopped at the bay's mouth;
all he had seen in 1794 was solid ice.

During the century following Vancouver's visit, the glaciers
had receded; Muir and Young would be Glacier Bay's first
thorough explorers. Their excitement grew with each dip of the
paddle. Huge icy chasms and battlements glared down at them
as they slowly moved up the ice-choked bay; savage winds
blew. Of the many coastal inlets they had seen, this was by far
the iciest, the wildest, the most raging—and therefore the most
alluring. Yosemite-like canyons still in the making yawned on
either side. Awesome rivers of ice ended in avalanches. Whale-
size ice chunks plunged seaward, breeding huge waves and
swells, and endless fleets of icebergs streamed out to sea. The
slowly receding glaciers left in their wake a land totally wild
and newborn, scraped clean of vegetation.

"The only signs of former life were the sodden and splin-
tered spruce and fir stumps that (Continued on page 149)

"...the most startling, chilling, almost shrieking vitriol blue..."

Gaping crevasses plunge deep into Reid Glacier, dwarfing a hiker climbing on the jumbled ice at the glacier's end. Such rivers of ice form in areas receiving heavy snowfall. Pressure gradually turns the snow to ice, and its vast weight—accumulated over long years—propels it slowly downhill.

Mist shrouds the waterfront of Wrangell as a motorboat glides across its quiet harbor. "Wrangell was a tranquil place," wrote Muir. "I never heard a noisy brawl in the streets, or a clap of thunder, and the waves seldom spoke much above a whisper along the beach." Starfish (left) cluster in a tidal pool near town. Settled in 1834 by Russian fur traders, Wrangell subsequently prospered under the English and then the American flags. During the Klondike Gold Rush of 1898, Wrangell served as a way station and trading post to miners heading north. Still a small town, Wrangell today has one of Alaska's largest sawmills.

Canada geese take wing from tidal flats off Admiralty Island. Muir sheltered here: "The rain, bitterly cold and driven by a stormy wind, thrashed us well while we floundered in the stumpy bog trying to make a fire...."

projected here and there from the bases of huge gravel heaps," Young reported. These trees had been leveled by ancient glacial advance, and preserved in ensuing floods of water and mud. But, Young added, even in the plowed-over barrenness of Glacier Bay, Muir "saw design in many things which the ordinary naturalist overlooks, such as the symmetry of an island, the balancing branches of a tree, the harmony of colors. . . ." He also marveled at mosses, lichens, and other pioneer plants — the first citizens of this bare, virgin ground that had known no vegetation, no sunlight for thousands of years.

The same plants still clothe those parts of Glacier Bay most recently uncovered by retreating ice. They mingle with the relic trees in an intriguing juxtaposition — the living mosses and dead stumps are two consecutive populations, sharing the same earth but separated by 5,000 years of ice.

Muir loved Glacier Bay and its "mountaineering of the most trying kind." He camped on some of its glaciers, rambled their fragmented surfaces, even mapped, sketched, and named a few. But, as it turned out, he was not the bay's discoverer. Unknown to him, U. S. Navy Lieutenant C. E. S. Wood had briefly entered Glacier Bay in 1877, two years before. Muir, however, was the first to explore it extensively and to popularize it. He sought out battlefronts between rock and ice as if possessed: "The grandeur of these forces and their glorious results overpower me and inhabit my whole being. Waking or sleeping, I have no rest. In dreams I read blurred sheets of glacial writing, or follow lines of cleavage, or struggle with the difficulties of some extraordinary rock-form." Glacier Bay became Muir's laboratory and schoolroom, where he rose before dawn to explore daylong, pointing out glacial action to Young.

"Somehow a glacier never seemed cold when John Muir was talking about it," Young wrote. Eagerly he absorbed the glacial lessons, and even "learned from Muir the gentle art of sleeping on a rock, curled like a squirrel around a boulder."

Muir and Young roamed Glacier Bay for a week, braving fogs and the sleep-shattering "ice-guns" of glaciers as they calved icebergs. Then the sun finally poked through the heavy overcast, illuminating Mount Crillon — the highest peak they could see — with a surreal glow. Young recalled: "It was not sunlight; there was no appearance of shining; it was as if the Great Artist with one sweep of His brush had laid upon the king-peak of all a crown of the most brilliant of all colors."

To Muir, the mountain seemed "thrust into the body of the sun itself." Downward burned this "supernal fire," until "every mountain was apparently glowing from the heart like molten metal fresh from a furnace." Slowly the light faded to normal intensity. Declared a "hushed and awe-stricken" Muir: "We have met with God!"

Never again would John Muir be totally content with the

Perched atop a Sitka spruce, a bald eagle surveys the countryside near the narrow fiord of Tracy Arm. An endangered species, bald eagles thrive in southeastern Alaska; wildlife specialists have counted more than 750 nesting pairs of bald eagles on Admiralty Island alone — the largest concentration in the United States.

American West; Alaska, especially Glacier Bay, had a firm grasp on his heart. Although he would resume life in California, he would revisit the northland five more times, entranced by its savage beauty of ice and rock sculptures, its hugeness, its grand totality of power.

He next returned in 1880, propelled by a desire to find his way among the icebergs of Sum Dum Bay. Again he went by red-cedar canoe, with Young and Indian guides. The Tlingits by now had made Muir an honorary chief during a tribal ceremony; they dubbed him "Great Ice Chief," a title Muir cherished almost as much as he did Alaska's "noble, newborn scenery."

The second Sum Dum expedition found icebergs again jamming the inlet. But this year, Muir persisted, waiting for a flood tide to sweep the ice back toward the head of the bay; he entered unobstructed.

NEARLY A CENTURY LATER, Farrell and I used the same strategy to ease our way through the ice-filled waters of Tracy Arm, one of Holkham Bay's two tributary fiords. The intervening years would give us an edge over Muir. We were armed with tide schedules, two guides, and a couple of hundred pounds of gear carried in a floatplane.

As we approached the narrow, curving inlet, sharp mountains poked through the hemlock and spruce forest. Icebergs liberally dotted the water, reminding us of Muir's experience here: a "fine lot of Sum Dum ice,—thirty-five or forty square miles of bergs." Our pilot somehow found an opening in all that white, and we landed.

We unloaded quickly and set about assembling the pair of two-man kayaks, puzzling together slender struts and braces, then stretching the canvas over them, as if pulling on huge socks. Soon we four were off, course set for the head of Tracy Arm and Muir's "lost glacier" of 1879.

Sunlight bounded off the water and ice-polished rock walls. Frothy cascades streaked cliffs that angled sharply. Already, Muir's descriptions of this canyon were holding true. "Headland after headland, in most imposing array, was seen plunging sheer and bare from dizzy heights, and planting its feet in the ice-encumbered water." Tracy Arm's numerous cliffs and side canyons so captivated Muir that he sped from one to the next like a child let loose in a toy store.

He described the icebergs as "azure caves and rifts of ineffable beauty, in which the purest tones of light pulse and shimmer, lovely and untainted as anything on earth or in the sky." Young was less favorably disposed. "They are treacherous creatures, these icebergs. You may be paddling along by a peaceful looking berg, sleeping on the water as mild and harmless as a lamb; when suddenly he will take a notion to turn over, and up under your canoe will come a spear of ice, impaling it and lifting it and its occupants skyward; then, turning over, down will go canoe and men to the depths."

I mulled over that chilling warning as the bergs of Tracy Arm crowded increasingly about our fragile craft. Icebergs are especially awesome when viewed from water level in a kayak. Even the tiniest chips of ice loom threateningly. A few of them snuggled a bit too close; the scratchy rasp of ice on canvas sounded alarmingly like tearing cloth—I imagined a sharp stiletto of ice slitting our kayak as a fisherman might gut a salmon. But both boats sturdily survived.

Muir's fascination with icebergs persisted to the head of Tracy Arm, where "berg after berg was being born with thundering uproar" from the channel's main glacier.

"There is your lost friend," said his Indian guides. "Your friend has *klosh tumtum* [good heart]. Hear! . . . he is firing his guns in your honor."

Muir reached the Tracy glacier in a single afternoon; yet even after two days of canoeing we had seen no sign of it. The reason, of course, is that the glacier has receded many miles since Muir's visit. Finally, on the evening of the second day, we rounded a bend and confronted two glaciers—flanking an island never mentioned by Muir. Evidently, the single ice river of his day had withdrawn back to two tributary branches, its retreat leaving that small bit of land uncovered. We put ashore on the island and found it so recently glaciated that even mosses had had little opportunity to homestead. A few hardy trees had taken root, one holding the nest of a bald eagle—complete with two fuzzy eaglets.

From the topmost rock of the island, I gazed about at a primal scene. To the left was the crooked fiord we had paddled up, its 4,000-foot-high walls chiseled into a smooth U-shaped gateway by the ice. On the right loomed one jagged glacier; straight ahead rose the other. Domed mountains fell sharply to the sea all around. Offshore, the mournful howls of seals echoed among the ice floes; eagles drifted high above; glaciers periodically boomed. My senses were overpowered by this majestic display of wildness, and at the variety and sheer size that is Alaska. I understood Muir's devotion to this land.

His love of glaciers later focused on a particularly large and active ice sheet in Glacier Bay; it measured perhaps a mile and a half across and reared its head some 700 feet above the water. Muir drove stakes into it, revisiting them on several occasions to gauge the glacial movement. In some places, according to Young, he found that the glacier advanced 50 or 60 feet a day. Within a year, that glacier was named for Muir.

Today, Muir Glacier is retreating, as are some of the other 16 tidewater ice sheets in Glacier Bay. Its motion is especially speedy—about three feet daily, the fastest ice retreat ever recorded. The glacier's snout lies 20 miles inland from where Muir first saw it, less than a century ago.

"To dine with a glacier on a sunny day is a glorious thing," Muir once wrote while traversing his namesake. That same day, however, the fierce glare of reflected sunlight drove him nearly snow-blind. He fell into a crevasse filled with icy water; he dragged himself out and might have perished had he not stripped on the spot and somehow "shivered away the night" without catching pneumonia.

On a later hike across Muir Glacier, a hike shrouded by cold, misty rains, John Muir became lost—one of the few times that ever happened; only a fiery beacon set by his Indian friends brought him to camp. "The glacier almost got me this time," he admitted. But his enthusiasm had never dimmed. Stumbling into camp about midnight, he ate some hot food—the day's first—and glowingly recounted his adventures to Young.

"Man, man; you ought to have been with me. You'll never make up what you have lost to-day. I've been wandering through a thousand rooms of God's crystal temple. I've been a thousand feet down in the crevasses, with matchless domes and sculptured figures and carved icework all about me. Solomon's marble and ivory palaces were nothing to it. Such purity, such color, such delicate beauty!"

When Muir was warned by his physician to avoid Muir Glacier or risk death from an illness, he stormily replied that if he did not go, he would surely die. Like mountains, glaciers seemed to hold curative powers for his ills. Although a severe bronchial cough had plagued him for three months, he trekked across the glacier in 1890, at age 52. The ice was so rugged that he wore out the new soles of his boots during the week-long trip. "I intended to camp on the glacier every night, and did so," he reported, "and my throat grew better every day until it was well, for no lowland microbe could stand such a trip." Muir's understandable pride in his hardiness and endurance moved him to observe of himself in his old age, "I have made a tramp of myself. I have gone hungry and cold. I have left bloody trails on sharp ice peaks to see the wonders of the earth!"

His last visit to Muir Glacier—and Alaska—came in 1899, as a member of the Harriman Alaska Expedition. This milestone voyage was organized by railroad magnate Edward H. Harriman, one of Muir's lifelong friends. The expedition conveyed 25 leading American scientists along 9,000 miles of Alaska's shores, from Wrangell through the Alexander Archipelago, the Gulf of Alaska, the Aleutian Islands, and all the way to the Bering Strait. It was a trip of great discovery; numerous stops permitted comprehensive, firsthand studies of the land, its life forms, its native societies. In addition to a large crew, the boat carried scientific gear, stenographers, a 500-volume library—

"everything such an expedition could possibly need," said John Burroughs, one of the scientists. To feed his guests, Harriman stocked his floating laboratory with eleven live steers, and flocks of sheep and poultry. "The hold of our ship looked like a farmer's barnyard," Burroughs remarked.

Also on board was the Harriman family. Eldest son W. Averell Harriman—destined to become one of America's most honored and durable statesmen—still vividly recalls that voyage, made when he was only seven years old. I visited him in the memento-filled study of his home in Washington, D. C. Slim and craggy at 84 years, Mr. Harriman said that of all the important and influential people on that voyage, two individuals clearly stood out—John Muir and John Burroughs.

"They were alike in two respects," he told me. "One was their rather long beards—which naturally impressed a child of my age—the other was their tremendous interest in and dedication to conservation. I always think of them as being together, very attached to each other."

They were similar also in build, age, and heritage. Scottish blood bred a matched pair of tempers, and each loved to take verbal jabs at the other. Burroughs nicknamed his colleague "Cold-Storage Muir" for his unfailing love of ice, applauding him as "an authority on glaciers, and a thorough one—so thorough that he would not allow the rest of the party to have an opinion on the subject."

But even Burroughs—an easterner—could not escape a Muir-like attraction for Alaska's beauty. On deck one evening to view the alpenglow, he was joined by Muir. "You ought to have been here fifteen minutes ago, instead of singing hymns in the cabin," chided Burroughs. "Aye," sniffed Muir, "and you, Johnny, ought to have been up here fifteen years ago, instead of slumbering down there on the Hudson!"

Averell Harriman described another Muir quality: "I've a clear recollection of his gentle kindliness. He was outgoing with children, interested in us. I had a very affectionate regard for him. He would talk about his interests in different subjects. And quite delightfully."

During the evenings, expedition members alternated in giving talks or telling stories. Muir's best-remembered contribution was a tale about S. Hall Young's dog—a ragtag mongrel named Stickeen.

At first, Muir had crustily disdained Stickeen as a "contrary little vagabond." But the dog sought him out, "forsaking . . . even his master to share my wanderings." Before a week had passed, Stickeen's victory was complete; he slept at Muir's feet, and accompanied him on rambles, even across dangerously crevassed glaciers. He seemed to relish the very wilderness delights that Muir most prized. "Once he followed me over a glacier the surface of which was so (Continued on page 158)

Muskegs—boggy, brownish meadows among the trees—harbor a luxuriant growth of vegetation near Wrangell. Spongy, highly absorbent sphagnum moss forms the foundation of a muskeg, often extending dozens of feet into the ground; constantly decaying flora adds to the thick soil. Stunted spruces sprout from the mossy blanket amid pools of tannin-stained water. "I never saw a richer bog and meadow growth anywhere," said Muir of Alaska's muskegs. Graceful plants flourish on the banks of the Stikine River, where Muir spent long hours collecting flowers. Sundew plants (above) extend sticky-tipped arms that trap insects; shooting stars (upper left) explode with color; fungi (below left) thrive on rotting tree bark; a skunk cabbage opens its yellow sail.

Stylized face glares from a totem pole in
Wrangell; Muir found totems "the most
striking of the objects displayed here." With
knives and chisels, Tlingit Indian craftsmen
fashioned such sculptures from tree trunks
to tell legendary tales, memorialize their
dead, and display their clan emblems. The
400 people who live in Angoon (above)—a
native village on Admiralty Island—still
cling to many of their traditional ways.
Following a Tlingit custom, the family of
Jimmie Johnson, chief of the Raven clan,
honored his memory by temporarily
closing his house when he died. After a
brief period, clan members will open the
house and renovate it for his family.

THE LORD IS MY SHEPHERD
JIMMIE JOHNSON
BORN JUNE 16, 1879
"GONE TO BE WITH THE LORD"
FEB 15, 1978

crusty and rough that it cut his feet until every step was marked with blood; but he trotted on with Indian fortitude until I noticed his red track, and, taking pity on him, made him a set of moccasins out of a handkerchief. However great his troubles he never asked help or made any complaint, as if, like a philosopher, he had learned that without hard work and suffering there could be no pleasure worth having."

It was on a later glacial trip that "a wild storm was blowing and calling, and I could not wait." Muir left camp in early morning to hike across a seven-mile-wide glacier; he soon noticed Stickeen close behind.

The storm quickly worsened. "Instead of falling, the rain, mixed with misty shreds of clouds, was flying in level sheets, and the wind was roaring as I had never heard wind roar before." Still, Muir and Stickeen traversed the glacier in about three hours, finding it level and fairly free of crevasses. They explored a side glacier, planning to return by way of the "grand crystal prairie" they had crossed that morning. But somehow they followed a different route—one that led to "a maze of crevasses of appalling depth and width." Carefully Muir picked the way, leaping smaller gaps and finding ice bridges across the larger ones. Stickeen bravely followed.

But a fast-dropping sun caught the pair suddenly face-to-face with a yawning crevasse—an abyss perhaps 40 feet across. Searching up and down its length, Muir found only one overpass—a giant razor of ice spanning the crevasse diagonally, "the very worst of the sliver bridges I had ever seen. It . . . extended across from side to side in a low, drooping curve like that made by a loose rope. . . . But the worst difficulty was that the ends of the down-curving sliver were attached to the sides at a depth of about eight or ten feet below the surface of the glacier." With his ice ax, Muir chopped steps down the wall, then straddled the sliver "like a boy riding a rail fence" and hitched himself forward an inch or two at a time. He planed down the sharp edge of the bridge as he crossed, leaving it about four inches wide for his companion. On the far side, he rose to his feet, and "with infinite pains cut narrow notch steps and finger-holds" in the almost vertical wall. "At such times one's whole body is eye," wrote Muir. "How I got up that cliff I never could tell. The thing seemed to have been done by somebody else."

Mimicking the sacred Raven, other animals, and mythical monsters, Tlingit Indians entertain Muir in the large blockhouse of their chief, Shakes. After dining on canned food—a delicacy to the natives—the Indians made the explorer an honorary chief. Muir, later named "Great Ice Chief," described the dancing as "a monotonous stamping accompanied by hand-clapping, head-jerking, and explosive grunts kept in time to grim drum-beats."

But what of Stickeen? So far he had been totally fearless: "nothing seemed novel to him, nothing daunted him," vouched Muir. With this treacherous crevasse, however, "poor little Stickeen was crying as if his heart was broken, and when I called to him in as reassuring a voice as I could muster, he only cried the louder."

A heart-to-heart conversation finally convinced the dog that he must try to follow Muir's footholds down the wall. He "pressed his body against the ice as if trying to get the advantage of the friction of every hair, gazed into the first step, put his little feet together and slid them slowly, slowly over the edge and down into it, bunching all four in it and almost standing on his head." Again and again he repeated the process down to the icy razor, then padded hesitantly across "as if holding his breath, while the snow was falling and the wind was moaning and threatening to blow him off." But the worst still lay ahead; at the sheer uphill wall "I feared he might fail, for dogs are poor climbers." Ten vertical feet of ice lay between the two adventurers. When Muir reached down to help, Stickeen "was looking keenly into the series of notched steps and finger-holds I had made, as if counting them, and fixing the position of each one of them in his mind. Then suddenly up he came in a springy rush, hooking his paws into the steps and notches so quickly that I could not see how it was done, and whizzed past my head safe at last!

"And now came a scene! 'Well done, well done, little boy! Brave boy!' I cried, trying to catch and caress him; but he would not be caught. . . . He flashed and darted hither and thither as if fairly demented, screaming and shouting, swirling round and round in giddy loops and circles like a leaf in a whirlwind, lying down, and rolling over and over, sidewise and heels over head, and pouring forth a tumultuous flood of hysterical cries . . . all the time screeching and screaming and shouting as if saying, 'Saved! saved! saved!' "

So popular was this tale of Stickeen that Muir eventually enlarged it into a book. To him, the perils encountered on that chilling razor of ice would ever remain "the most memorable of all my wild days."

Those wild days in the wilderness of Alaska underlined again to Muir the importance of preserving the heritage of such lands throughout the United States. With renewed determination, he returned to California to further the most important contribution of his life—conservation.

"The sky opened and the blessed sun shone out over the beautiful waters and forests with rich amber light," wrote Muir at the end of an Alaska storm; a rainbow arches skyward after a heavy rain near Admiralty Island. Light and color fascinated Muir with the natural paintings they created.

6

"THE HOPE
OF
THE WORLD"

Corrugated bark sheathes the trunks of coast redwoods, rising more than 200 feet in Muir Woods National Monument near San Francisco. "This is the best tree-lover's monument that could be found in all the forests of the world," wrote Muir of this woodland, named in his honor in 1908. Gentle animals, as well as mighty trees, captivated Muir; he sketched the rabbit above in a journal.

"IN GOD'S WILDNESS lies the hope of the world," John Muir preached, with a fervor that came straight from his heart. All his life, Muir lauded nature's beauty; every forest yawned before him "beautiful and sublime." But his love of trees stemmed from practical reasons as well as esthetic ones. Years in the Sierra had taught him the vital role of forests in creating and maintaining watersheds: Destroy the trees and you destroy California's agriculture in the valleys below, he warned. He became an ardent and vociferous conservationist, firm in the belief that "wildness is a necessity," not just a luxury for the backcountry rambler.

"Heaven knows that John the Baptist was not more eager to get all his fellow sinners into the Jordan than I to baptize all of mine in the beauty of God's mountains," he would say. Such evangelism came late to Muir, who grew up, basically, as a loner. Though he realized the joys of nature even as a boy, he was content long into adult life just to savor such joys in solitude and silence, ignoring those who could not hear nature's call.

Only upon entering middle age did he evolve into a crusading author eager to spread his wilderness gospel. This conversion—as decisive as the shop accident that blinded him or the bout of malaria that turned his feet toward California—would eventually exert an impact on an entire nation, an impact unmatched by that of any other American naturalist. Muir's emergence was sluggish, stalled by self-doubt. When Emerson and others first urged him to write articles, he shyly replied, "What I have nobody wants. Why should I take the trouble to coin my gold? Some will say it is Fool's Gold."

His sole writings in his early years consisted of letters and journal notes—bits of vividly informative and impromptu prose scribbled in the privacy of nature and never intended for a publisher's eyes. Finally, in 1871, his friends' persistent pleadings won out; Muir redrafted some old letters into a summary of his glacial theory and sent the piece to the *New York Tribune*. To his amazement it was published, paid for, and followed by requests for more!

Muir quickly progressed from articles on Sierra glaciers to other nature writings, then to entertaining yarns of Yosemite life—all presented in the humorous fashion of a Mark Twain or Bret Harte. The easygoing style, however, belied the difficulties Muir experienced. Unlike speech—his preferred medium— writing grated against his temperament. Always he rebelled at formality; the knowledge that thousands would read his words choked early efforts with a monumental writer's block. He strained for phrases; veins popped out on his hands—but not a sentence reached the blank page.

"I find this literary business very irksome," he complained, damning it as "the life of a glacier, one eternal grind." Help arrived in the form of friend John Swett, who advised Muir to

"Write as you talk." Slyly, he would draw Muir into a conversation on the day's adventures, await the inevitable flood of words, and then direct the author back to his writing room.

The method worked; Muir soon had some 15 articles in preparation. He became a contributor to the western magazine *Overland Monthly*. The *San Francisco Evening Bulletin*, *Scribner's Monthly*, and *Harper's Magazine* all published him. Muir began to spend his winters in San Francisco, writing.

Muir's prose often rambled as much as his feet, ranging from scientific measurements of glacial motion to flowery descriptions. Nevertheless, his writings always exuded a characteristic enthusiasm for the wilds, an enthusiasm so boundless that the editor of *Atlantic Monthly* wrote to Muir after reading one manuscript: "I felt almost as if I had found religion!"

Between bouts of writing, Muir ran off to the mountains to renew his creative thrusts in these "fountains of men as well as of rivers." He returned from each trek like Moses from Mount Sinai, driven by an unquenchable urge to enlighten his fellow man. "I am hopelessly and forever a mountaineer . . . and I care to live only to entice people to look at Nature's loveliness," he wrote a friend. He strove to be "a flake of glass through which light passes," focusing and transmitting to his readers the simple truth of wilderness. Often, he wrote at John Swett's house in San Francisco, a happy home where other boarders—including artists and writers—helped generate a creative atmosphere. Muir realized that writing meant he could no longer be a full-time mountaineer; he already felt the "hooks of civilization." But it was this very civilization that must hear his gospel—and besides, he enjoyed his new role as wilderness sage. After four decades spent in nature's heart, he was tiring of having no home but the great night sky. Even Emerson had warned him: "Solitude is a sublime mistress, but an intolerable wife."

Jeanne Carr, wife of Dr. Ezra Carr, who had befriended Muir at the University of Wisconsin, deserves much credit for the socialization of John Muir. She had helped him meet Emerson, artist William Keith, and others of similar intellect. She continually encouraged his writing. Also, she introduced him to Louisa (Louie) Strentzel, daughter of horticulturalist Dr. John Strentzel, who owned a sprawling fruit ranch near Martinez, east of San Francisco.

On April 14, 1880, John Muir married Louie, and became even more settled. Friends congratulated him on becoming "a member of the human family." He would live on the Strentzel ranch, and become its overseer.

The day after his marriage, Muir went straight to the orchards. His combination of Scottish business sense and plain hard work soon boosted the ranch to peak production. Muir grafted Dr. Strentzel's more than a hundred varieties of pears and grapes onto the highest quality and most desirable strains.

Muir managed the ranch so profitably that he eventually tucked away several savings accounts, one of which topped $50,000. Bankers looked forward to regular appearances of the lank, bearded man who carried his deposits in a large white laundry bag.

For nearly a decade, Muir devoted himself to horticulture and making money, setting aside in that time enough to ensure permanent support for his wife and their two daughters—Wanda and Helen—and to permit his own early retirement. Although the ranch brought financial independence, it also demanded much time and hard work. No longer could he actively preach conservation, or savor the embrace of mountains that had sparked his enthusiasm. The dusty orchard rows sapped his strength and burdened his spirit—and all but killed his writing talents. Even though he and Louie had long agreed that each summer would be his to ramble the highlands, such wilderness intervals proved all too brief. Muir's constitution deteriorated; his weight plummeted to a hundred pounds. And so, harvest time or not, Louie decided that he must regain his "wilderness health." She wrote to her mother, "He must not leave the mountains until he is well and strong again."

Repeated "rebaptisms" in sharp mountain air soon healed Muir's physical ills. They also shocked him with scenes of growing devastation. He lamented that "the glory is departing," after seeing the forests of Mount Shasta laid waste by timbering. Painfully, Muir watched as lumbermen dynamited sequoias, and sheep plundered virgin meadows throughout the Sierra. Speculators and monopolies had grabbed the richest California land and were developing it at great profit, with little consideration for its beauty or ecological importance. To them—and to most Americans of their day—wilderness was nothing more than a vast reservoir of raw materials awaiting man's pleasure. Their quick destruction of the land stoked Muir's fires of protest; his desire and ability to write returned. He realized that nature's only chances for survival lay in protection through proper legislation and changes in public attitudes. Muir would generate both.

Already, friends had pleaded with him to head the rising conservation movement. Then old ally Robert Underwood Johnson, now an editor of the influential Century Magazine, galvanized Muir's efforts. In 1889, the two visited Yosemite, viewing with horror the ruination of meadows and forests, both in the Valley—then a state park—and in the high country surrounding it. Near Tuolumne Meadows, Muir found the forest floor "bare as the streets of San Francisco," and even the young trees "eaten out of existence by hoofed locusts." Johnson proposed that they work together to make a national preserve of the high country that enclosed the Valley. He knew important people in Washington who could start a bill in Congress at the opportune time; it would be up to Muir to argue the conservationist's cause before the American public.

Muir did. At Johnson's suggestion, he wrote two articles for *Century* that ably convinced readers of the vital need to protect still-pristine Yosemite highlands, prime watershed of the state. In 1890, those lands gained the cloak of federal protection through the creation of Yosemite National Park. General Grant National Park, a small grove of sequoias, and Sequoia National Park—both in the southern Sierra—were created in the same year. Muir and Johnson had precipitated a wave of national concern over the future of America's "Big Trees."

By this time, Louie had reached a decision: "A ranch that needs and takes the sacrifice of a noble life, or work, ought to be flung away...." At once she freed her husband of all ranch cares. Conservation would be his overriding concern.

Muir the conservationist arrived at a crucial period in America's history—following the squandering of resources in the East but before the final taming of the West. He realized—at a time when land seemed unlimited—that virgin tracts of land in the West must be protected. Largely because of his efforts, Yosemite, Rainier, Grand Canyon, Petrified Forest, and parts of the Sierra all became national preserves—and Muir became a major force behind our national park system.

Such an epitaph, alone, would satisfy most conservationists. But Muir achieved much more. He worked for passage of The Enabling Act of 1891, under which President Benjamin Harrison set aside 13 million acres of forest and, later, President Grover Cleveland protected 21 million acres more. When politicians threatened to abolish these reserves, Muir rallied conservationists with a classic appeal that appeared in the *Atlantic Monthly*: "Any fool can destroy trees. They cannot run away; and if they could, they would still be destroyed,—chased and hunted down as long as fun or a dollar could be got out of their bark hides, branching horns, or magnificent bole backbones...." The forest preserves remained inviolate.

In 1892, Muir further bolstered the cause of conservation by helping to create the Sierra Club, whose main purpose still is "to enlist the support and cooperation of the people and government in preserving the forests and other natural features of the Sierra Nevada Mountains." Muir became its first president, and held the post for life. Under his direction, the Club grew into the guiding light for conservation, generating national awareness of ecology, calling for wilderness preserves, and battling those who despoiled America's natural wealth.

Muir's first book—*The Mountains of California*—was published two years after the founding of the Sierra Club, bringing him another success that solidified a growing nationwide desire to conserve. By then, Muir had settled into a writer's daily regimen, rising early in his (Continued on page 176)

"Come to the woods, for here is rest…. The squirrel will come and sit upon your knee…."

Centuries-old sequoia dominates surrounding firs in Sequoia National Park. Muir often meandered through such woodlands, discovering a kinship with forest creatures such as the ground squirrel above. "Going to the woods is going home," he said.

"The feathery boughs are extended above my head like hands of gentle spirits."

Outspread branches of a fir tree evince the symmetry and grace of nature so admired by Muir; he would sit in a forest for hours and reflect on the beauty around him. In such wildernesses he would find intricate patterns in bits of nature. Clockwise from top left: the jigsaw-puzzle bark of a ponderosa pine; the soft colors of new growth and immature cones; seeds and scales of a cone scattered by a squirrel; and the cross-section of a fir cone.

Time-twisted Sierra juniper clings to a rocky cliff in the Sierra Nevada. The sublime beauty of trees like the towering sequoia at right, and wildlife like the Steller's jay, perpetually lured Muir to the mountains. "Another glorious Sierra day. . . ," he wrote. "Life seems neither long nor short, and we take no more heed to save time or make haste than do the trees and stars. This is true freedom, a good practical sort of immortality. . . ."

"Any fool can destroy trees."

Bleached roots of a fallen sequoia form a mazelike pattern. Muir considered death as beautiful and as necessary as life—when it came naturally. But when caused by man, it angered him. The stump of a sequoia cut nearly a century ago stands like a gravestone in Kings Canyon National Park. Muir spoke sharply against misuse of America's land and resources—dynamiting sequoias for lumber, carving petrified wood into souvenirs, timbering Sierra slopes to make hayfields. His written and verbal appeals helped rouse citizens and politicians into establishing a system of national parks and forests that would preserve some of the nation's most beautiful wildernesses.

Martinez home and going upstairs to the large "scribble-den." Books and a dozen different manuscripts littered the room — until daughter Helen got him to tie red ribbons around completed articles and drop them in a fruit box so she would know which ones to type.

His low, simple oak desk remains today, preserved along with the entire home as the John Muir National Historic Site. Some 30,000 visitors annually make the pilgrimage to this Muir shrine, roaming through the 17 rooms of molded plaster ceilings, marble fireplaces, and redwood paneling, all designed in grand Victorian manner by Muir's father-in-law. One Muir alteration — a brick fireplace — might clash with the stylish decor, but it often warmed its owner with "a real mountain campfire" in the bosom of civilization.

Muir's bedroom still lacks drapes, because he preferred the sun, not servants, to wake him. Mottled window glass softens the view of a gas station, power lines, and freeways that currently infringe on the serene manse, cradle of Muir's most famous writings. All of his books took shape there, as did his strategies for furthering the conservation movement. Quotes now mounted about the house remind visitors of his all-consuming purpose: "The battle for conservation will go on endlessly. It is part of the universal battle between right and wrong." Another reads: "It is blessed to lean fully and trustingly on Nature, to experience the infinite tenderness and power of her love."

Crowning Muir's Martinez home is a glassed-in cupola some six feet square. Here, Muir often spent the early-morning hours, contemplating the countryside that is now suburban sprawl. But even with the surrounding changes, it is hard to climb those worn steps and not experience visions of an old man standing at the windows, gazing silently out at his dawn-drenched fields and — more likely — toward the east, the direction of the distant Sierra.

Muir's books furthered his reputation as nature's chief spokesman. And so, in 1903, when newly-elected President Theodore Roosevelt — himself greatly concerned over land management in the West — decided to see Yosemite, he took John Muir as his personal guide and companion.

"I want to drop politics absolutely for four days, and just be out in the open with you," he wrote to Muir. Although officials and local residents had planned to entertain their honored guest in style, Roosevelt preferred Muir's simple ways, camping out with him first in Mariposa Grove, then near Glacier Point without tents, or even cots. One morning they woke beneath a four-inch blanket of snow. "This is bullier yet!" Roosevelt crowed. At last, there was a politician who appreciated nature — and Muir.

Muir lost no time transmitting his love of the Sierra to the

Waterfalls cascade down sheer canyon walls in
Yosemite's Hetch Hetchy Valley, sketched by
Muir about 1900. For a decade, Muir fought
to save the valley from being dammed and
flooded to provide a reservoir for San Francisco. Although he lost the battle—engineers
completed O'Shaughnessy Dam (right) in 1923
—his struggle helped to spur the public into
an awareness of conservation issues.

President, arguing that only federal protection could save Yosemite Valley from mismanagement and overgrazing. Such a
move meant that California—legal protector of the Valley—
would have to cede the area back to the federal government.
Roosevelt agreed that the Valley should become a federal preserve. In 1906, Yosemite Valley and Mariposa Grove became a
part of Yosemite National Park.

In 1909, President William Howard Taft visited Yosemite—
and also relied on Muir as wilderness confidant. He left similarly convinced of the need for conservation; his Administration
would consistently support Muir's stance.

John Muir might have promoted his cause—and career—
even more had he made regular lobbying trips to Washington,
but wilderness called too strongly. It remained his first love
long after marriage, settling down, and his subsequent emergence as a crusading author. "I . . . am always glad to touch the
living rock again and dip my head in high mountain sky," he
wrote. Naturalist John Burroughs once said of his good friend,
"He could not sit in a corner   (Continued on page 184)

177

Amid scattered manuscripts, a thoughtful John Muir writes in his home at
Martinez, California. Here, Muir penned many of his most influential books
and articles. In 1880, at age 41, he married Louisa Strentzel, daughter of a
wealthy orchard owner in Martinez, and settled down to manage his
father-in-law's ranch (above). With his wife and daughters, Wanda (left)
and Helen, Muir sat for a portrait on his front porch about 1904. Wanda
fondly recalled that "Father was the biggest, jolliest child of us all."

Lofty palms and golden grasses surround the main house at the John Muir National Historic Site in Martinez. The 17-room home re-creates the style of the Muir household, including the "scribble-den" (above) and the girls' bedroom. For the first years of his marriage, Muir devoted himself to work in the ranch's orchards, gaining a sizable fortune and showing a sharp business sense. But mountains and the conservation movement always beckoned, and, with the blessing of his family, he again turned his attention to traveling, writing, and speaking.

Seeking advice on conservation programs, Presidents Theodore
Roosevelt and William Howard Taft each traveled to Yosemite
to meet John Muir. Above, Roosevelt and Muir stand on
Glacier Point across from Yosemite Falls in 1903. The two
camped for several days in the wilderness; Muir underlined
the need for federal protection of America's forests and scenic
wonders. "I stuffed him pretty well regarding the timber
thieves, and the destructive work of the lumbermen, and other
spoilers of the forests," recalled Muir. The Roosevelt
Administration created five national parks, 23 national
monuments, and added more than 148 million acres of
woodland to the national forest system. At left, reporters,
politicians, and soldiers surround Muir and President Taft in
1909 as they sit in a stagecoach near a tunnel in the trunk of a
sequoia. Muir gained the President's support in the fight to
save Hetch Hetchy, but lost the battle after Taft's term ended.

of the landscape, as Thoreau did. He must have a continent for his playground." And sometimes, even a continent would not suffice. "The world's big," Muir said, "and I want to have a good look at it before it gets dark."

Muir's desire to wander drove him on worldwide excursions, first to Europe in 1893, then to Asia in 1903, and finally to South America and Africa eight years after that. Before leaving for Europe, he attended several New York champagne parties given in his honor. Here he met Mark Twain, Rudyard Kipling, and other notables—and was surprised to be so well known in the East. Following a quick pilgrimage to Walden Pond and the graves of Emerson and Thoreau, he set off.

Europe's mountains, glaciers, and wilderness greatly pleased Muir, whose main problem was language. His French bore such a terrible accent that he wrote home: "Even the dogs don't understand it as I speak it, and refuse to wag their tails...."

The South American voyage, made in 1911—more than four decades after Muir's initial attempt to see the Amazon—finally fulfilled his youthful dream to "be a Humboldt!" He threaded through the lush Amazon basin, wondering at the giant ferns and vines and dense, tangled groves of araucaria trees—a "Magnificent primeval forest." Long had this savior of the sequoias yearned to see the world's *other* big trees, and now, finally, he was doing just that. In Africa he sought out and found the contorted baobab. "Kings may be blest, but I am glorious!" wrote the white-haired sage, effervescent over "one of the greatest of the great tree days of my lucky life."

Between these global wanderings, Muir vigorously continued to carry the banner of conservation. One of the most important battles of this time was over Hetch Hetchy, a stupendous valley just north of Yosemite.

"A grand landscape garden, one of Nature's rarest and most precious mountain temples," he had dubbed this meadowed and high-walled paradise that resembled Yosemite Valley in remarkable detail. William Keith, the artist, considered Hetch Hetchy's charms even superior to Yosemite's! Its autumnal splendors so transfixed him that he sketched it dozens of times in a single season. Since 1871, Muir had known and loved Hetch Hetchy, writing about it in *Overland Monthly* and other publications. But now the forces of progress were bent on turning this idyllic mountain valley into a reservoir to hold water for San Francisco, 200 miles away.

"Dam Hetch Hetchy!" Muir stormed. "As well dam for water-tanks the people's cathedrals and churches, for no holier temple has ever been consecrated by the heart of man."

The struggle over Hetch Hetchy dragged on for ten years as Muir marshaled his talents and the Sierra Club to defeat "these temple destroyers" who "seem to have a perfect contempt for Nature, and, instead of lifting their eyes to the God of the mountains, lift them to the Almighty Dollar." He urged his readers to see the mountain joys of Hetch Hetchy for themselves. He pointed out—as did a report from the Advisory Board of Army Engineers—that alternate water supplies could be developed outside the Park. Other sources, Muir argued, were available "in a dozen different places."

Muir's work had convinced both the Roosevelt and Taft Administrations to keep the valley intact. But in 1913, incoming President Woodrow Wilson appointed Franklin Lane, an avowed dam proponent, as his Secretary of the Interior. The bill that would remove Hetch Hetchy from the protection of Yosemite National Park and hand it over to San Francisco—a bill long delayed in Congress by its own backers because they awaited a favorable administration—was pushed through the House of Representatives when many members were absent.

Again John Muir set about rousing the forces of conservation, hoping to defeat the bill in the Senate or Oval Office. But despite his most urgent writings and speeches, the bill became law. Hetch Hetchy was lost.

To Muir, this was the single most tragic of all man's abuses of nature, one that meant the destruction of a wild valley as dear as Yosemite itself. Even today, 63 years after the defeat, a few residents still recall Hetch Hetchy's glory. Eleanor Sell Crooks, who has known Yosemite since childhood, remembers "grass up to the horses' stomachs in Hetch Hetchy, and a big rock just like El Capitan with waterfalls. It was beautiful. My mother said that if there hadn't been a Yosemite park, Hetch Hetchy would be it." Talk of a dam "started a big ruckus," she added. "My folks were very upset—it was all so unnecessary."

But unnecessary or not, O'Shaughnessy Dam—named for the man who directed its construction—eventually plugged the Tuolumne River, flooding Hetch Hetchy. As a final insult, the valley's trees were felled for timbers to make the dam. Its rocks were crushed into gravel for concrete.

The lake created by O'Shaughnessy Dam is today an important source of water and power for San Francisco. At the invitation of the San Francisco Public Utilities Commission, I joined watershed keeper Leon Elam for a cruise of the reservoir, which seemed serene almost to the point of ghostliness. We were alone on the lake, not another person visible anywhere. But the peace one might expect from such solitude eluded me. I felt instead an eerie uneasiness, prompted by the inescapable fact that I was gliding 80 feet *above* the flowery meadows Muir lauded and sought to save. Only 80 feet away, but I could not see them or even visualize them. Eighty feet, in fact, was "about as close as anyone ever gets" to the valley floor, Leon told me on that chill April day. "We've had a very late winter this year —no spring melt yet. If the water drops much more, we'll have to shut off the turbines."

Already the lake had fallen 220 feet from peak level, leaving the reservoir filled to only one-ninth of its capacity. Though the low mark concerned Leon, I silently welcomed this opportunity to see more of Muir's Hetch Hetchy than is usually visible. Many streams and waterfalls trace the fractured, glacier-polished canyon walls that still jut above water. But even while I gazed at their beauty, my eyes could not ignore the clashing ugliness that accompanies the reservoir's seasonal low mark. A broad, indelible bathtub ring lines the dark gray canyon with a slash of white, water-bleached rock. And on several sandy flats bared by the receding water, bleak groves of tree stumps littered the land. They jolted my senses, devastating any first impressions of serenity, for I suddenly realized those remnant trees were leafy and alive in Muir's lifetime. They remain a physical, tangible link to the man who loved them as living forests, and who mourned their desecration.

The threat of the drowning of this valley heralded sad days for John Muir, who feared the defeat might spur opportunists to challenge other national parks as well. His grief and the exhaustion of a desperate, decade-long fight had sorely taxed his health. Worse, he found himself increasingly alone. Louie had died, as had John Swett, Jeanne Carr, William Keith, and Edward Harriman—he had buried all his closest friends. Yet Muir's will to endure somehow reasserted itself: "We may lose this particular fight, but truth and right must prevail at last. Anyhow we must be true to ourselves. . . ." He found the strength to look on his victorious enemies with the patience a parent might show disobedient children: "They will see what I meant in time. There must be places for human beings to satisfy their souls. Food and drink is not all. There is the spiritual. In some it is only a germ, of course, but the germ will grow!"

Grow it did, nurtured in part by a burgeoning national shock over the loss of Hetch Hetchy. Muir's beloved valley became the Alamo of the conservation movement. New national parks were quickly established, along with the National Park Service that would administer them. Muir had advocated the creation of just such a department for many years, but the idea did not become a reality until 1916. By then, Muir was dead, gone to some "higher Sierra."

JOHN MUIR'S DEATH came just a year after the final struggle over Hetch Hetchy, on the day before Christmas, 1914. That was also the year in which the last passenger pigeon died; the species that a youthful Muir had envisioned "flying in vast flocks that darkened the sky like clouds" now was extinct.

With Muir's death, old friend S. Hall Young penned, "I cannot think of John Muir as dead. . . . He was too much a part of nature—too natural—to be separated from his mountains, trees, and glaciers." Muir's grave lies not in the mountains, however, but about a mile from his Martinez home, on private land. Here, awash in a sea of green that old-timers call "miner's lettuce," lies the low, plain slab topped by a single engraved flower—a Scottish thistle designed by Muir. It is a simple memorial to a man who left America such an immense legacy. But then our national parks and forests, the Sierra Club, and the simple fact that wilderness exists—all serve as living memorials to Muir's work and life.

Petrified Forest National Park holds a "grove" of petrified trees that Muir discovered and named; Muir Woods National Monument, a preserve of coast redwoods just north of San Francisco, symbolizes his crusade for the sequoias; the John Muir National Historic Site at Martinez recalls the years of writing and struggle; Muir's name on many California trails and peaks reaffirms his importance to wilderness and conservation. A photograph of the white-haired visionary continues to reign over the Sierra Club headquarters in San Francisco, enabling its founder to live on visibly as well as in spirit. Club president Kent Gill acknowledged some changes since Muir's day—most notably the Club's expansion from strictly Sierra concerns to global ones, including such urban troubles as pollution. "We got into pollution for the same reasons that Muir fought for the Sierra—he was concerned with the whole, and believed that all things are related." And so, Gill believes, "If John Muir came back today, he'd probably nod his head and smile—I think he'd like what we've done, what we're doing."

Across San Francisco Bay from the Sierra Club, the John Muir Institute for Environmental Studies fosters research and educational projects that concern ecology. Other groups also bear Muir's name, and proudly. Yet with all this homage, one glaring omission remains: There is no John Muir National Park.

Muir's many followers intended in the late 1930's to name a proposed national park south of Yosemite for him. What better memorial could there be to the man who had most loved these mountains and who had crusaded for their preservation? But Muir's opponents prevailed, and a campaign to discredit him resulted in a last-minute change of titles. In 1940, the preserve became Kings Canyon National Park and absorbed the existing General Grant grove of sequoias.

"California and the Government owe him penance at his tomb," raged Robert Underwood Johnson. Well, yes, penance might help. But Muir remained, lifelong, a simple man, more often disposed to shyness than self-acclaim. Perhaps the best penance of all would be total individual immersion in nature, following Muir's "wildest, leafiest, and least trodden" ways. Muir, I think, would prefer that.

It was in this frame of mind that I joined 14 Sierra Club

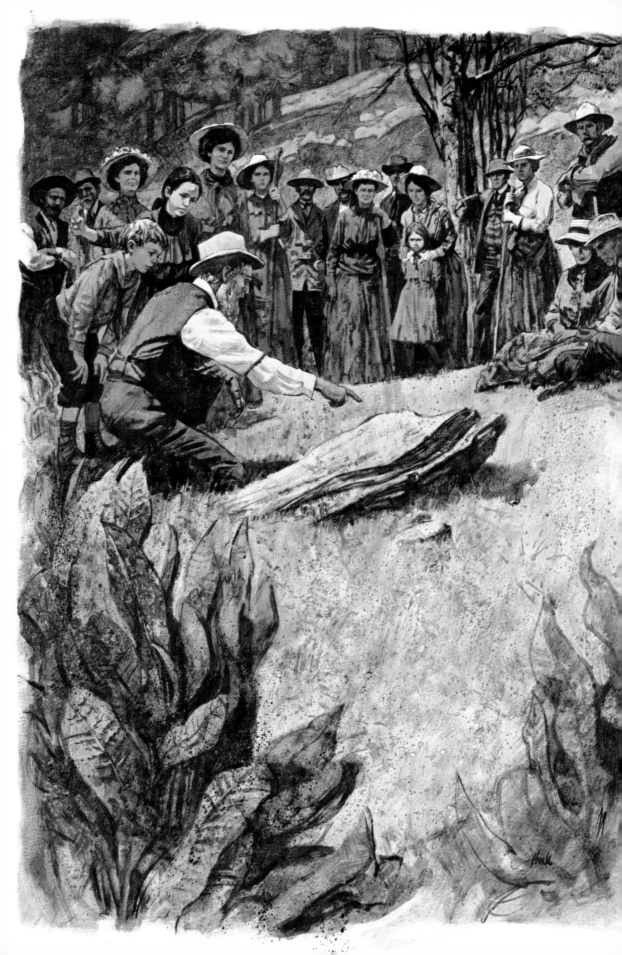

members bent on sampling the winter beauty of Grand Canyon National Park. Unlike most Park visitors who hew to the developed South Rim, we would hike to the very bottom of the Canyon during a six-day backpack, leaving comfort and civilization far behind. Our guides would be the resident wildlife—feral burros and remnant herds of mountain sheep—that continue to scratch a system of rough trails in the Canyon's dusty surface, trails that even today provide the best routes of ascent and descent in wilder portions of the Park.

Muir's first visit to Grand Canyon left him awed. "It seems a gigantic statement for even nature to make, all in one mighty stone word." Praise flowed nonstop from his pen. "We oftentimes see Nature giving beauty for ashes—as in the flowers of a prairie after fire—but here the very dust and ashes are beautiful. . . . Wildness so godful, cosmic, primeval, bestows a new sense of earth's beauty and size." The scale of the Canyon amazed Muir: "It is very hard to give anything like an adequate conception of its size; much more of its color, its vast wall-sculpture, the wealth of ornate architectural buildings that fill it, or, most of all, the tremendous impression it makes."

This awesomeness remains today, of course. My approach to the Canyon was from the south, across flat Arizona countryside uniformly dusted with sagebrush and some winter snow. Suddenly, with no warning whatever, I came to that huge, ragged gash, its edge dropping sheerly and suddenly for more than a mile. Here, rim-to-rim distances gape as wide as ten miles. Innumerable side canyons and drainages radiate from the main furrow, adding greatly to its variety and dimension. Muir observed, ". . . were you to trace the rim closely around on both sides, your journey would be nearly a thousand miles long." Truly, this canyon is grand.

Happily, canyon treks have the advantage that—in a refreshing departure from mountain climbs—one sets out downhill, greatly easing the weight of a full pack. Still, we twisted and bowed through the scrubby juniper and piñon pines, avoiding prickly pear and sharp-edged yucca leaves that can painfully slash an unwary hand. Sliding, ever-crumbling rock underfoot added further challenge. Our need for water and the Canyon's scarcity of it dictated strenuous, daylong hikes if we were to camp each night beside a water source. Even then, we made two dry camps. Mileages became meaningless amid the vast convolutions we followed. It took a full day to tramp from Royal Arch to Elves' Chasm—though the straight-line distance is barely a quarter of a mile! But such minor rigors were richly repaid with endless vistas of natural rock sculptures. Their size, their beauty, inspire the mind to wonder.

Just the majesty of five sunsets and sunrises viewed from within the Canyon made our 70 miles afoot worthwhile. Though we started each day wrapped (Continued on page 194)

Venerable sage of the mountains, John Muir explains the effects of glaciation on a rock in Yosemite to three generations of wilderness enthusiasts. "Never was there a naturalist who could hold his hearers so well, and none had so much to tell," remarked one such follower of Muir. The legacy of John Muir endures today —in the lands he helped protect, in his writings on nature and conservation, and in the spirit of freedom he discovered in the wilds.

"...Grand Canyon...a gigantic statement for even nature to make...."

Clouds mass in a darkening sky as a storm approaches the South Rim of the Grand Canyon in Arizona. Overwhelmed by the awesomeness of this gorge, Muir wrote: "Wildness so godful, cosmic, primeval, bestows a new sense of earth's beauty and size." Muir encouraged Theodore Roosevelt to protect the Grand Canyon; it became a national park in 1919. Below, a petroglyph in Arizona southeast of the Grand Canyon depicts running animal figures. Indians of the Southwest carved them in weathered sandstone more than 500 years ago.

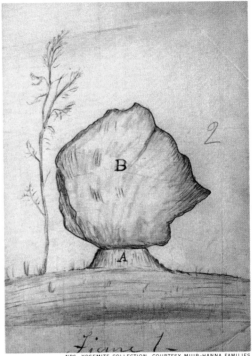

Colored by time, petrified logs lie scattered on the desert floor at Petrified Forest National Park in Arizona. Nearly 200 million years ago, water and mud blanketed fallen logs here; minerals slowly replaced wood cells and turned the logs to stone. The variety of minerals produced the different whorls of color (above left). John Muir—who discovered one group of these logs—probed the mysteries of the Petrified Forest with the same boundless curiosity that prompted him to sketch a large balanced boulder.

in the dark shadow of this natural cleft, light from a sun yet unseen set the opposite rim magically aglow. Reflections back and forth among the highest crags spawned a host of early-morning hues and gigantic, ever-moving shadows. Light, we discovered, is as basic to the Canyon as is stone. It changes constantly, blooming then fading on distant peaks, filling a grotto for one brief interlude, casting sculptures in deep shade, bleaching ravined plateaus into one sunny, dimensionless flatness. Each morning's unfolding festival of light and rock tempted me to watch it from one spot for the entire day, as Muir loved to do.

But I could not. Our next destination beckoned; a full day of walking followed each dawn. An occasional evening campfire eased tired limbs as it chased, temporarily, the descending cold. We fifteen crowded round it, trading tales. We were a mixed group: a San Diego architect and his two children, a high-school track coach who jogged daily even here, a salesman, a Midwestern grandmother—all strangers brought together by a shared love of wilderness.

"There's more to life than money," stated one of the group, a 44-year-old assembly-line worker. He maintained that, rather than a pay raise every year, he would prefer "more time off to do the things I really want to do"—such as ramble in a wilderness. Others readily agreed, displaying a spiritual bond with the Scottish-born naturalist who valued nature's own comforts above material ones. These modern members of the Sierra Club —whether they knew it or not—were all following some of Muir's oft-repeated advice:

> Keep close to Nature's heart, yourself;
> and break clear away, once in a while, and
> climb a mountain or spend a week in the
> woods. Wash your spirit clean. . . .

In such words—and in such monumental preserves as Grand Canyon—the legacy of John Muir endures.

"When we contemplate the whole globe as one great dewdrop, striped and dotted with continents and islands, flying through space with other stars all singing and shining together as one, the whole universe appears as an infinite storm of beauty," wrote John Muir. He viewed the universe as a grand harmonious whole, and he visualized his own place in the cosmos with the signature (above) scrawled in an early travel journal.

INDEX

Boldface indicates illustrations; *italic* refers to picture captions

196

Library of Congress C̄ĪP̄ Data

Melham, Tom, 1946-
 John Muir's Wild America.

 Bibliography: p. 199
 Includes index.
  1. Muir, John, 1838-1914. 2. Wilderness areas—United States. I. Grehan, Farrell. II. National Geographic Society, Washington, D. C. Special Publications Division. III. Title.
 QH31.M9M37 333.7′2′0924 [B]
 76-687 ISBN 0-87044-186-8

The Special Publications Division is grateful to the individuals, organizations, and agencies named or quoted in the text and to those cited here for their generous cooperation and assistance during the preparation of this book: Harvey Arden, National Geographic Staff; William F. and Maymie B. Kimes; Shirley Sargent; Jack Gyer, Curator of Yosemite Collections; Staff of the Stuart Library, University of the Pacific; Stanwyn G. Shetler, Associate Curator, Department of Botany, Smithsonian Institution; Jean Hanna Clark; Richard R. Hanna; the National Park Service and the staffs of Grand Canyon, Mammoth Cave, Mount Rainier, North Cascades, Olympic, Petrified Forest, Sequoia-Kings Canyon, and Yosemite National Parks, John Muir National Historic Site, Glacier Bay and Muir Woods National Monuments; the National Forest Service and the staffs of Shasta-Trinity, Stanislaus, and Tongass National Forests; the Smithsonian Institution.

Books by John Muir: *Letters to a Friend, The Mountains of California, My First Summer in the Sierra, Our National Parks, Picturesque California and the Region West of the Rocky Mountains, from Alaska to Mexico, Steep Trails, Stickeen, The Story of My Boyhood and Youth, Studies in the Sierra, A Thousand-Mile Walk to the Gulf, Travels in Alaska, The Yosemite.*

William F. Badè, editor, *The Life and Letters of John Muir,* Volumes I and II; Dave Bohn, *Glacier Bay: The Land and the Silence;* John Earl, photographer, *John Muir's Longest Walk;* Francis P. Farquhar, *History of the Sierra Nevada;* Kay Gresswell, *Glaciers and Glaciation;* Frederic R. Gunsky, editor, *South of Yosemite;* Aubrey L. Haines, *Mountain Fever: Historic Conquest of Rainier;* Holway R. Jones, *John Muir and the Sierra Club;* Shirley Sargent, *John Muir in Yosemite;* Smithsonian Institution, *Harriman Alaska Expedition,* Volumes I and III; Edwin Way Teale, editor, *The Wilderness World of John Muir;* Robert L. Usinger and Tracy I. Storer, *Sierra Nevada Natural History;* Linnie Marsh Wolfe, *John of the Mountains* and *Son of the Wilderness: The Life of John Muir;* S. Hall Young, *Alaska Days with John Muir.*

National Geographic books: *Wilderness U.S.A.; The New America's Wonderlands, Our National Parks;* William R. Gray, *The Pacific Crest Trail.* Readers may also want to consult the National Geographic Index for related material.

Composition for *John Muir's Wild America* by National Geographic's Phototypographic Division, Carl M. Shrader, Chief; Lawrence F. Ludwig, Assistant Chief. Printed and bound by Kingsport Press, Kingsport, Tenn. Color separations by Colorgraphics, Inc., Beltsville, Md.; Graphic Color Plate, Inc., Stamford, Conn.; Progressive Color Corp., Rockville, Md.; J. Wm. Reed Co., Alexandria, Va.

JOHN MUIR'S
AMERICA

Glacier Bay,
Alaska

Totem Poles,
Wrangell, Alaska

Half Dome,
Yosemite Valley, California

Martinez,
California

Grand Canyon, Arizona

Petrified Forest, Arizona